Researching Ancestral Crisis in Ireland

FAMILY HISTORY FROM PEN & SWORD BOOKS

Birth, Marriage & Death Records
The Family History Web Directory
Tracing British Battalions on the Somme
Tracing Great War Ancestors
Tracing History Through Title Deeds
Tracing Secret Service Ancestors
Tracing the Rifle Volunteers
Tracing Your Air Force Ancestors
Tracing Your Ancestors
Tracing Your Ancestors from 1066 to 1837
Tracing Your Ancestors Through Death Records – Second Edition
Tracing Your Ancestors Through Family Photographs
Tracing Your Ancestors Through Letters and Personal Writings
Tracing Your Ancestors Using DNA
Tracing Your Ancestors Using the Census
Tracing Your Ancestors Using the UK Timeline
Tracing Your Ancestors: Cambridgeshire, Essex, Norfolk and Suffolk
Tracing Your Aristocratic Ancestors
Tracing Your Army Ancestors
Tracing Your Army Ancestors – Third Edition
Tracing Your Birmingham Ancestors
Tracing Your Black Country Ancestors
Tracing Your Boer War Ancestors
Tracing Your British Indian Ancestors
Tracing Your Canal Ancestors
Tracing Your Channel Islands Ancestors
Tracing Your Church of England Ancestors
Tracing Your Criminal Ancestors
Tracing Your Docker Ancestors
Tracing Your East Anglian Ancestors
Tracing Your East End Ancestors
Tracing Your Family History on the Internet
Tracing Your Female Ancestors
Tracing Your First World War Ancestors
Tracing Your Freemason, Friendly Society and Trade Union Ancestors
Tracing Your Georgian Ancestors, 1714–1837
Tracing Your Glasgow Ancestors
Tracing Your Great War Ancestors: The Gallipoli Campaign
Tracing Your Great War Ancestors: The Somme
Tracing Your Great War Ancestors: Ypres
Tracing Your Huguenot Ancestors
Tracing Your Insolvent Ancestors
Tracing Your Irish Family History on the Internet
Tracing Your Jewish Ancestors
Tracing Your Jewish Ancestors – Second Edition
Tracing Your Labour Movement Ancestors
Tracing Your Legal Ancestors
Tracing Your Liverpool Ancestors
Tracing Your Liverpool Ancestors – Second Edition
Tracing Your London Ancestors
Tracing Your Medical Ancestors
Tracing Your Merchant Navy Ancestors
Tracing Your Northern Ancestors
Tracing Your Northern Irish Ancestors
Tracing Your Northern Irish Ancestors – Second Edition
Tracing Your Oxfordshire Ancestors
Tracing Your Pauper Ancestors
Tracing Your Police Ancestors
Tracing Your Potteries Ancestors
Tracing Your Pre-Victorian Ancestors
Tracing Your Prisoner of War Ancestors: The First World War
Tracing Your Railway Ancestors
Tracing Your Roman Catholic Ancestors
Tracing Your Royal Marine Ancestors
Tracing Your Rural Ancestors
Tracing Your Scottish Ancestors
Tracing Your Second World War Ancestors
Tracing Your Servant Ancestors
Tracing Your Service Women Ancestors
Tracing Your Shipbuilding Ancestors
Tracing Your Tank Ancestors
Tracing Your Textile Ancestors
Tracing Your Twentieth-Century Ancestors
Tracing Your Welsh Ancestors
Tracing Your West Country Ancestors
Tracing Your Yorkshire Ancestors
Writing Your Family History
Your Irish Ancestors

Researching Ancestral Crisis in Ireland

A Guide for Family Historians

CHRIS PATON

Pen & Sword
FAMILY HISTORY

First published in Great Britain in 2025 by
PEN AND SWORD FAMILY HISTORY
An imprint of
Pen & Sword Books Ltd
Yorkshire – Philadelphia

Copyright © Chris Paton 2025

ISBN 978 1 03611 037 6

The right of Chris Paton to be identified as Author of this work has been asserted by him in accordance with the Copyright, Designs and Patents Act 1988.

A CIP catalogue record for this book is available from the British Library.

All rights reserved. No part of this book may be reproduced, transmitted, downloaded, decompiled or reverse engineered in any form or by any means, electronic or mechanical including photocopying, recording or by any information storage and retrieval system, without permission from the Publisher in writing. No part of this book may be used or reproduced in any manner for the purpose of training artificial intelligence technologies or systems.

Typeset by Mac Style
Printed in the UK by CPI Group (UK) Ltd, Croydon, CR0 4YY.

The Publisher's authorised representative in the EU for product safety is Authorised Rep Compliance Ltd., Ground Floor, 71 Lower Baggot Street, Dublin D02 P593, Ireland. www.arccompliance.com

For a complete list of Pen & Sword titles please contact

PEN & SWORD BOOKS LIMITED
47 Church Street, Barnsley, South Yorkshire, S70 2AS, England
E-mail: enquiries@pen-and-sword.co.uk
Website: www.pen-and-sword.co.uk
or
PEN AND SWORD BOOKS
1950 Lawrence Road, Havertown, PA 19083, USA
E-mail: uspen-and-sword@casematepublishers.com
Website: www.penandswordbooks.com

CONTENTS

Introduction — vii
Acknowledgments — xiii
Timeline — xiv

Chapter 1   Irish Family History Research Basics — 1
    Births, Marriages and Deaths — 2
    Church Records — 4
    Census Records — 7
    Wills — 8
    DNA Testing — 9
    Gateway Sites — 11
    Irish Archives — 12
    British Archives — 15
    Libraries — 16
    Commercial Vendors — 17
    Newspapers — 22
    Societies — 25
    Commercial Research Services — 26

Chapter 2   Family Events and Relationships — 28
    Births and Illegitimacy — 29
    'Fallen Women' — 34
    Mother and Baby Homes — 40
    Foundlings — 43
    Orphans — 46
    Adoption — 48
    Child Migrants — 51
    Marital Issues — 52
    Separation and Divorce — 56

Bigamy	61
Homosexuality	63
Death	67
Suicide	71
Chapter 3 Law and Order	**75**
The Brehon Laws	75
English Law	77
The Crown Courts	78
Local Courts	81
Grand Juries	83
Manor Records	84
Church Courts	87
Police and Prison Records	89
Transportation	93
Executions	96
Chapter 4 Poverty and Health	**102**
The Poor Law	103
Deportation of Irish Paupers From Britain	110
Hospitals and Public Health	112
Asylums	118
Chapter 5 Them and Us	**124**
The Plantations of Ulster	124
The 1641 Rebellion	126
The Cromwellian Conquest	130
The Penal Laws	130
The Great Famine	131
The Land War	134
The Home Rule Crisis	135
The Suffragettes	137
The Dublin Lockout	138
The First World War	140
The Easter Rising	142
The War of Independence	144
The Treaty and the Civil War	146
The Legacy of Conflict	149
Further Reading	151
Index	153

INTRODUCTION

One of the greatest challenges that we all face when carrying out our Irish family history research is to venture beyond the basics of who was hatched, matched and despatched using the vital records, and to try to find out more about our ancestors as living, breathing individuals. Many factors can get in the way of such pursuits, from limited or lost documentation, to the dreaded 'what do you want to know that for?'

When we look in a mirror, we may gain a partial glimpse of our forebears, for we inherit some of their physical traits, even if we don't know which bits we may have inherited from whom. But it is not enough for us to establish a meaningful connection, and we remain curious about them beyond the basic facts of their names and dates. We may wonder how they prospered while at school, what their hobbies were, who their friends and enemies might have been, what their politics and/or religious beliefs were, what made them laugh and cry, what their physical and mental wellbeing was like, and so on. The more that we can answer such questions, the stronger the connections that we may feel with them become, and the ability to empathise with events that led to us becoming who we are today.

No matter how idealistic we may wish their lives to be, however, it is often the case that we discover their stories may not necessarily have been all sweetness and light. Our ancestors were no different to us in experiencing hardship at times, and although we may wish the best for them as their descendants, we may need to remove our rose-tinted glasses to get to the truths and consequences of their actual lives as lived.

When I commenced my research into the lines of my parents (both of whom are now sadly passed), I started with what I already knew as a base line. I knew that they had separated from each other in 1978 when I was just 8 years of age. Although Irish born, at the time I was living in Plymouth, England, where my father had been serving in the Royal Navy; within months of their separation, our family had all left our comfortable house in Laira Green, and returned to my parents' home town in Carrickfergus, County Antrim.

To be pragmatic, our parents divided their children between them to be raised, with the eldest two, myself included, taken on by my father. My father's mother had recently passed away, with my father inheriting her house, and thus it was to be that for my first two years in Carrick (as it was known locally) I lived in her house with my father. The building had no interior bathroom, and contained just a single tap to provide cold water, meaning many nights of bathing while standing in a basin of water that had just been heated on the gas cooker. That was the easy part – to go to the toilet we had to cross the back yard to visit an outside based privy, always a fun endeavour in the middle of a snowy winter.

When I started to investigate my ancestry, I soon discovered that in some ways history had repeated itself. Both of my parents informed me that their own sets of parents had also separated when they were young. The parents of my father Colin (1945–2021), Charles Paton and Jean Currie, did so when he was just a young boy aged about 5. At one stage, he remembered his mother coming into his bedroom one night, kissing him on the forehead and saying, 'Remember your mother always loves you', and this being the last he would see of her for a couple of years. Jean, originally from Scotland, took her daughter Sheila with her over the Irish Sea to Auchterarder in Perthshire, having got a job there as a domestic servant at the local Gleneagles Hotel, famous for its golf course. My father, along with his two older brothers, was left behind in Belfast to be raised on the Sandy Row by his father. Two years later, Jean returned from Scotland to take custody of all four children, at which point she moved the family to nearby Carrickfergus.

My mother Charlotte (1950–2013), known to everyone as 'Cherie', had also witnessed a parent leaving the family home when she was just a child, and at about the same age. The story she recalled was that her father, Ernest Graham, a boilermaker, had left his wife, Martha Smyth, and moved to Cumberland in England for a few years, before relocating to Pembroke in Wales, where he took up residence at a hotel for many years. On one fateful day in 1972, he was told that a fellow employee had not turned up for work, and was asked if he minded covering for him. Unfortunately he agreed to do so; during his shift, the scaffolding on which he had been working on suddenly collapsed, with Ernest falling to his death.

Barring my grandfather's accident, which was reported in the press following a coroner's inquiry, there is little documentary evidence available to confirm the above anecdotes just outlined about my family – indeed, what you have just read may well be the only documented account ever recorded. I was able to find some evidence to corroborate parts of it, but it is the oral history passed down from my parents that has provided the backbone of my research.

As we go further back in time, however, it becomes much harder to find out about the everyday hardships faced by earlier generations, because those who could pass on their own oral testimonies are now long gone. Instead, we need to rely on any documented records left behind. If we are lucky, we might find a diary or some letters to provide us with a clue as to their 'voice', to offer a sense of who they were. For the most part, however, we may have to rely on the accounts of others who witnessed events in times of hardships.

The author's grandfather Ernest Graham, who was killed in an accident in Wales in 1972.

There are no rules in genealogy, but there are seemingly many truisms. If there is one area where we may be able to truly glean some insight into our ancestors' lives, it is when they experienced adversity. In such moments others were drawn into their contemporary world, some of them as witnesses armed with a quill and ink ready to document such scenarios for a variety of reasons. These scribes may have been part of the family circle – they may equally have been members of the judiciary, poor law officials, police officers, registrars, journalists, or any number of other possibilities. And through their words, we can open the door into the most extraordinary of circumstances.

Within the family environment, for example, there may have been many dramas. Children may have died in infancy. Some may have been born illegitimately, carrying what society defined as a stigma throughout their lives, while their mothers were treated as pariahs. Others may have been abandoned as foundlings, or perhaps given up for adoption, losing any sense of their original identity. For those who later married, there may have been strains on their relationships, affairs, separations, or a lifetime of misery trapped in a loveless union. Gay ancestors may have lived their lives in fear of the death penalty, perhaps marrying to hide their circumstances, with some being discovered and prosecuted.

In a society where the rule of law dominated, our ancestors may have fallen victim to crime, or may have been the criminals. They may have sought retribution in the courts, or faced prosecution – and if found guilty, may have been imprisoned, transported, or executed. For those found innocent, a stigma may still have followed a trial, with society continuing to shun them in its aftermath. Others may have been accused of vile acts or misdemeanours as a form of defamation, and punished for incidents of which they were entirely innocent. Did those prosecuted as witches in Ireland truly have access to dark powers, or did they simply not fit in, to be removed easily by an accusation of sorcery? There may have been issues also with poverty, debt and famine, as harvests failed, investments crashed, or as our ancestors' bodies inevitably began to fail them.

To try to explore such possibilities, whenever you come across a stated fact in a document, you first need to understand exactly what has been recorded, why it was recorded, and equally importantly, how it was recorded. You may, for example, find a birth registered for an ancestor, where the child is listed under the mother's surname, and with the father's name missing. What this will undoubtedly mean is that the mother was not married, and that the father had not consented to having his name registered in the record. But while this may reveal that the mother had her child out of wedlock, the record does not reveal the circumstances. Was the child borne of a simple one night stand, as part of an affair, or was the mother perhaps raped? Was the father still on the scene, or did he deny liability? If so, was he made to accept it?

Such a birth record will answer none of this, but there may be other clues and records to help discover the circumstances – and the father's identity. The child may have been given the father's surname in the birth record as a middle name, either in tribute or as an act of defiance. There may have been a case raised at the local church or civil courts to try to compel a putative father to step forward and contribute financially towards the upkeep of the child. If a serious violation of the mother had occurred, there may have been an investigation carried out, it may have been reported in the press, and there may have been a prosecution. If the father's identity can still not be determined, the child's very DNA legacy may still be present within the researcher seeking to find answers several generations later.

In other circumstances, a crisis situation may be more apparent. For example, you may find that a newspaper article notes an ancestor as having been prosecuted by the courts for a particular incident. But is that it on the documentary front? If a person was prosecuted, they had to be first investigated, arrested, interviewed, charged, taken before the courts, and sentenced, with the sentence then executed. At each stage of the process records will have been created, which may be held in local archives, or at the relevant national archive, which can help to further flesh out the story, and reveal more about the family concerned.

And what would be the impact of a prosecution? If the convicted person was the main breadwinner of the family, how did those now unsupported survive the period of their loved one's incarceration? Did they seek poor relief? Were they supported by other family members? Or did they themselves have to take up work to make up the shortfall? While the victims of a crime may have received justice, the relatives of the criminal may equally have become victims, shunned by the society that once embraced them, forcing them to retaliate or relocate. Some of this may be documented.

A word of caution though. As family historians, we can get excited about the discovery of such material. And yet no matter how fortunate we may be to find such evidence, and how delighted we may be to have done so, we should always bear in mind that what we have just uncovered is evidence of a story which may have caused no end of sleepless nights, tears, grief, punishments and more. Indeed, along the way we may even discover some things that we had not expected to find at all. Through DNA research, for example, it is entirely possible to uncover new family members, near and far, who were not a part of the official family narrative. We have a duty to be responsible with our finds, particularly those that may continue to carry a stigma or hurt for those still living today. And we absolutely need to respect the privacy of the present generation.

In an age where genealogical research increasingly seems to be developing into a pursuit of database hits to provide instant dopamine rushes, with little thought as to what is actually being found and revealed, the purpose of this book is to help the researcher step back and to take a fresh look at the stories being uncovered, placing them into context. Even for situations where specific records may not have survived, or may not be so easily accessible, topics will be covered to help provide a narrative context for the information that can be identified. It should be noted that Ireland does have a serious problem with lost documents, thanks to the destruction of the Public Record Office in the Civil War in 1922. Not everything was housed in the PRO, however, and unless you have confirmed that a record has not survived, the possibility of its existence needs to be pursued, for in some cases you will get lucky.

Throughout the book you will find detailed discussions about various records that can be used for research, with many cases studies thrown in for good measure, as drawn from years of engaging with collections both offline and online, including many from my own family's ancestry. Where records can be accessed online, these will be identified, but additional holdings in archives will also be flagged up. Along the way I will also add in some tips that may assist, with this being as good a place as any to give you the first one!

TIP: If a website appears to have died, try to find a stored or 'cached' version of it through the Internet Archive's free-to-access Wayback Machine at **https://web.archive.org**.

ACKNOWLEDGMENTS

As always, I have to thank a lot of folk who have helped with the creation of this book, including the good folk at Pen and Sword who have helped to pull the volume before you together, as well as my wife Claire, a constant source of joy and cups of coffee!

The book is first dedicated to the memory of my grandfather Ernest Graham, who I never got to know, he having died in that industrial accident in 1972, but whom I have since come to know more over the years from much that I have been able to discover about him.

But in particular it is dedicated to my sons Calum and Jamie, for whom I wish nothing but success and happiness at the start of their adult lives. No matter what life may throw at you in the decades to come, there will always be a way through, even if at first it does not present itself.

TIMELINE

The following timeline provides some key dates and events from the last five centuries in Ireland, which can act as a ready reckoner for genealogical and land history research.

Free State   Free State of Ireland/Saorstát Éireann
NI   Northern Ireland
ROI   Republic of Ireland

Pre-Union
1529   Tudor conquest commences
1556   Laois and Offaly plantations
1583   The plantations of Munster
1606   Hamilton-Montgomery settlements in Antrim and Down
1607   Flight of the Earls
1609   The plantations of Ulster
1641   Irish Rebellion
1649   Cromwellian conquest of Ireland commences
1702   Creation of the State Paper Office to hold records of the Lords Lieutenant of Ireland (the Crown's representatives in Ireland)
1702   Dublin Foundling Hospital established
1704   Act to Prevent the Further Growth of Popery
1707   Act to Prevent the Destroying and Murdering of Bastard Children
1708   Registry of Deeds established in Dublin
1730   First divorce case in Ireland (private act of Parliament)
1756   Dublin Magdalene Asylum founded
1774   Catholic Relief Act

1778	Catholic Relief Act
1791	First convict ship leaves Ireland for New South Wales
1793	Catholic Relief Act
1798	United Irishmen rebellion

Ireland in the United Kingdom

1801	Britain annexes Ireland to form the United Kingdom of Great Britain and Ireland
1821	First successful Irish national decennial census – few records survive
1823	Composition for Tithes Act; tithes now to be paid with money
1829	Roman Catholic emancipation; from this point, most Catholic parishes begin to keep registers of baptisms and marriages
1831	Decennial census – few records survive
1831–36	Tithe War
1832	Representation of the People Act
1835	First Report of Commissioners for Inquiring into the Condition of the Poorer Classes in Ireland
1838	Tithes Commutation Act; tithe rate reduced and incorporated into rent payments
1838	Poor Relief (Ireland) Act – creation of new state based poor law system
1841	Decennial census – few records survive
1845–52	Irish Famine (An Gorta Mór)
1845	Civil registration of non-Roman Catholic marriages commences
1846	Rateable Property (Ireland) Act – enabled Tenement Valuation (Griffith's Valuation)
1848	Young Ireland rebellion
1848	Encumbered Estates Act
1849	Encumbered Estates Act; Encumbered Estate Court established
1851	Decennial census – few records survive
1852	Landed Estate Court established
1852	Valuation (Ireland) Act – enabled publication of Griffith's Valuation
1857	Probates and Letters of Administration Act (Ireland)
1861	Decennial census – few records survive
1864	Civil registration of all births, marriages and deaths commences

1867	Fenian Rising
1867	Creation of the Public Record Office of Ireland
1868	End of convict transportation
1869	Home Children scheme devised in London
1870	Landlord and Tenant (Ireland) Act
1871	Disestablishment of the Church of Ireland (Irish Church Act 1869)
1871	Decennial census – few records survive
1877	Foundation of the National Library of Ireland
1879–82	Land War
1881	Decennial census – no records survive
1891	Decennial census – no records survive
1901	Decennial census – records have survived
1903	Land Purchase (Ireland) Act (Wyndham's Act); addressed absentee landlordism
1911	Decennial census – records have survived
1912	Signing of the Ulster Covenant
1914–18	First World War
1916	The Easter Rising
1919–21	The War of Independence
1920	Government of Ireland Act
1921	No decennial census carried out
1921	Partition of Ireland; creation of Northern Ireland and Southern Ireland
1921	First Dáil Éireann formed

Post Partition

1922	Irish Civil War – destruction of the Public Record Office of Ireland at the Four Courts
1922	Creation of the Free State of Ireland, and exit from UK
1923	Creation of the Public Record Office of Northern Ireland
1926	First post-Partition censuses in Northern Ireland and the Free State (Northern records have not survived)
1928	Legitimacy Act (NI)
1929	Adoption of Children (NI) Act
1931	Legitimacy Act (Free State)
1937	Constitution of Ireland; renames the Free State as 'Ireland' (Éire); Article 41 bans divorce
1937	Northern Ireland census – records have survived
1939	Matrimonial Causes Act (NI) – 'criminal conversation' cases end

1939	Second World War commences (The Emergency); National Identity Register (NI) created
1942	IRA Northern Campaign commences
1949	Republic of Ireland Act 1948 (Free State formally becomes a republic)
1952	Adoption Act (ROI)
1956	IRA Border Campaign
1969	The Troubles commence
1981	Family Law Act (ROI) – 'criminal conversation' cases end
1987	Status of Children Act (ROI) – removed status of illegitimacy
1988	Public Record Office of Ireland and the State Paper Office merge to form the National Archives of Ireland
1996	Last Magdalene Laundry closes (Sean McDermott Street, Dublin)
1996	Divorce legalised (ROI)
1998	Good Friday Agreement
2011	New PRONI building opens at Titanic Quarter, Belfast
2013	Taoiseach apologies for Magdalene Laundries
2015	Commission of Investigation into Mother and Baby Homes and Certain Related Matters established (ROI)
2015	Same sex marriage introduced (ROI)
2018	Legalisation of abortion (ROI)
2019	Legalisation of abortion (NI)
2019	Legalisation of divorce (NI)
2022	Birth Information and Tracing Act (ROI)

The counties of Ireland, and the Irish border.

Chapter 1

IRISH FAMILY HISTORY RESEARCH BASICS

Many people fail to engage with their Irish family history because of the oft quoted 'lack of records', referring to the opening actions of the Civil War in 1922 (p.146), when Ireland's national archive, the Public Record Office (PRO), was destroyed during the bombardment of the Four Courts complex adjacent to the River Liffey in Dublin. This incident led to the loss of hundreds of years of valuable documented insight into the nation's history. However, while it is true that the loss of these records will certainly be felt by every researcher trying to pursue their ancestry, it is absolutely not the case that this means that research cannot be carried out. It is important to note that the records destroyed at the PRO were only those held at the PRO – there are many other record sets that can assist which were never deposited in the archive in the first place. These include the state gathered civil registration records of births, marriages and deaths from the mid-nineteenth century, some church records, censuses, land records and more. Ireland had – and still has – more than one archive, and the researcher should consider that the glass is half full and not half empty when seeking to pursue their ancestral research.

In this chapter I will provide an insight into the basic records that can assist with research, then discuss some of the key archival institutions and websites that exist within and for Ireland. These tools should hopefully allow the researcher to create a basic genealogical tree against which the various topics of this book can then be measured against. A word of caution though – the information provided in records is only as good as the informant who supplied the relevant details in the first place, and the conveyance of such information is only as good as the scribes who were employed to write it all down.

A particularly useful resource for Irish research is the oral history record, the tales passed down through generations from one family member to another. Often the preservation of such stories can help to unlock tricky research problems, but again be wary. It may well be that a branch of the family emigrated to the United States following the Great Famine – but it might equally be that the Famine had nothing to do with it, and that the move was made for another reason that has long since disappeared from the folk memory. The truth, sometimes distorted, can often be found within such tales, providing occasional clues as to a family's plight.

For those based overseas beyond Ireland's shores, it is also worth bearing in mind that if you are only aware that your ancestors came from Ireland, and have little else to work with beyond that, you may initially find it difficult to make progress. Always check the documented resources in the areas where your ancestor emigrated to first in order to extract as much information as you possibly can about them there before you start. If possible, you really need to identify the religion of your forebears and from which particular part of Ireland they came, down to the parish, and if possible, even to the townland (a subdivision of a parish). If unsure of what can be plundered in your own area prior to a search, contact a local family history society or archive for advice (p.12); if still requiring help, assistance can be further sourced from professional researchers (p.26).

While the following will provide a basic insight, my books *Tracing Your Irish Family History on the Internet* (2nd edition), *Tracing Your Irish Ancestry Through Land Records*, and *Tracing Your Belfast Ancestors* go into considerably more depth on each topic, as well as many others. Another title, *Sharing Your Family History Online*, also provides a basic understanding of how to use your own DNA to make connections with distant relatives, although this is also briefly covered in this section.

Births, Marriages and Deaths

The civil registration of marriages in Ireland commenced in April 1845 for non-Roman Catholic marriages (i.e. for the various Protestant denominations, or for non-denominational marriages performed by the state's civil registrars), while all births, marriages and deaths were then supposed to be recorded from January 1864. Records were gathered in local registration offices, with copies sent to a centralised General Register Office for the whole of Ireland based in Dublin prior

Irish Family History Research Basics • 3

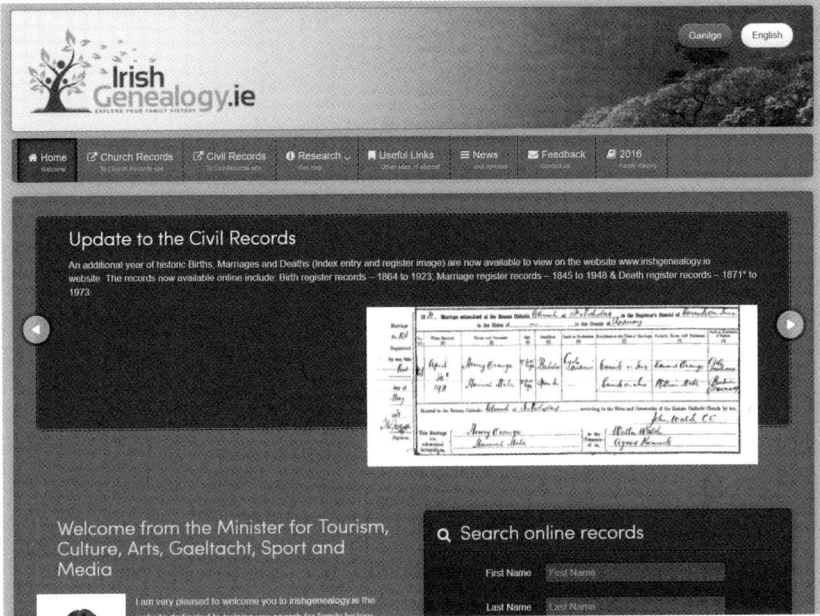

IrishGenealogy.ie provides free to access records for the whole of Ireland prior to Partition, and for the Republic thereafter.

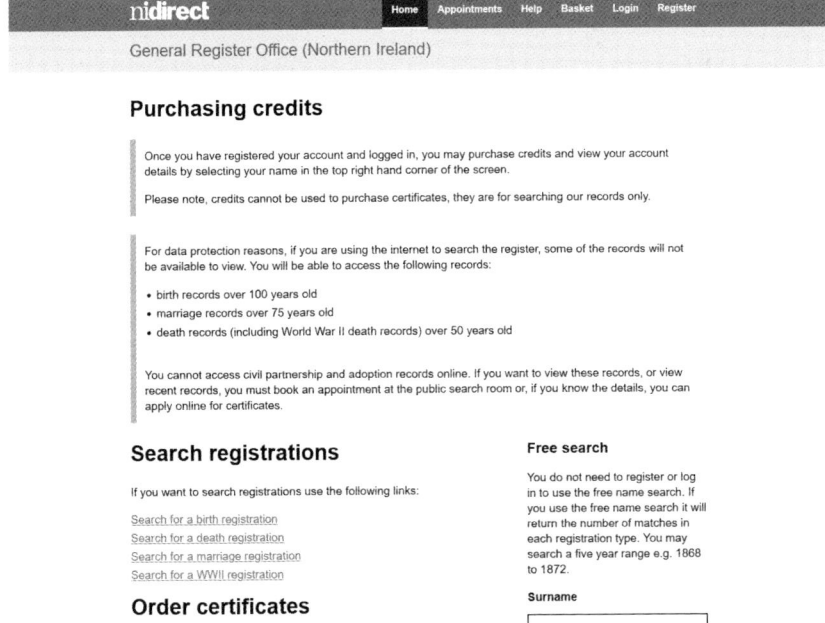

The GRONI website provides access to records for Northern Ireland only, including records following Partition.

to Partition. Today, there are two General Register Offices for Northern Ireland and the Republic of Ireland, located in Belfast (**www.nidirect.gov.uk/contacts/contacts-az/general-register-office-northern-ireland** and **https://geni.nidirect.gov.uk/Appointments**) and in Roscommon (**www.gov.ie/en/campaigns/af7893-general-register-office/**).

To find historical birth, marriage and death records online for the whole of Ireland before 1922, visit the free to access IrishGenealogy platform at **www.irishgenealogy.ie**. The site also hosts records for the Republic from 1922 onwards, but for Northern Ireland you will need to visit the pay-per-view **https://geni.nidirect.gov.uk**. Both sites have closure periods for online access, only providing access to birth records over a hundred years old, marriages over seventy-five and deaths over fifty. The information provided is as follows:

Births: Name, where and when born, the name of the father, his occupation and residence, the mother's name (including maiden surname), the name of the informant, and when and where registered.

Marriages: Where and when the marriage took place, whether civil or of a religious denomination, the names of both spouses, their ages (often noted simply as 'full' if 21 or over, or 'minor' if under 21), marital status, residence (often only the townland or town/city), the names of the spouses' fathers, their fathers' ranks or professions, the names of two witnesses, details of the celebrant, and where and when registered.

Deaths: The name of the deceased, where and when deceased, age at death, rank, profession or occupation, marital condition, certified cause of death, details of the informant, where and when registered.

Death records tend to be the least accurate at times, simply because the deceased was not the informant, but should still be sourced wherever possible.

It is also possible to visit research centres offering access to the records in both Belfast and Dublin, including more recent records not available online; for details on how to do so, consult the GRO websites noted above.

Church Records

For periods prior to the start of civil registration, or when civil records are not easily located, we need to rely on church records to try to discover when and where a child was born and/or baptised, the location and date of a marriage, and how, when and where a person died, and/or was buried.

The largest denomination on the island of Ireland has always been the Roman Catholic Church, but the state church prior to 1871 was in fact the Protestant based Church of Ireland, at which point it was disestablished from that role. The Church of Ireland was essentially the Church of England or Anglican Church in Ireland, but was just one of many Protestant denominations that has historically existed on the island; others have included the various Presbyterian denominations, the Methodist Church, the Baptist churches, and the Moravian Church. For a detailed oversight of the history of the main denominations, and the types of records that they generated, consult James G. Ryan's *Irish Church Records (New Edition)* (Flyleaf Press, 2001). For further information on the various different Presbyterian denominations, consult William J. Roulston's *Researching Presbyterian Ancestors in Ireland* (Ulster Historical Foundation, 2020).

The following are some online platforms providing access to digitised or historical records, or information on how to locate records.

Roman Catholic Records
Prior to 1829 not many Catholic parishes kept records due to the Penal Laws, although some registers do exist for certain areas. Even after emancipation in 1829, there are parts of the country where records were not kept until the 1830s, 1840s and even the 1850s. Note that Roman Catholic parishes may differ in name and have larger boundaries than the civil parishes used by the state for administrative purposes.

Catholic Parish Registers at the NLI (**https://registers.nli.ie**) contains digitised black and white microfilms of Catholic records from most Irish parish registers prior to 1881. The site does not contain indexes, and the digitised microfilms must instead be browsed; however, there are some filters that can steer you towards the relevant sets of records for a period within a particular microfilm.

While this site does not offer indexes, Ancestry (p.19) offers third party indexes to the same records through its 'Ireland, Catholic Parish Registers, 1655–1915' collection, which may help. Ancestry also has separate collections entitled 'Ireland, Select Catholic Birth and Baptism Registers, 1763–1917', 'Ireland, Select Catholic Marriage Registers, 1778–1942', and 'Ireland, Select Catholic Death and Burial Registers, 1767–1992'; these carry records only for a small number of parishes across the island, but where registers are offered they have been digitised in colour, and there

St Mary's Pro-Cathedral, Dublin. The Roman Catholic Church has historically been the largest religious denomination in Ireland.

is a longer range into the twentieth century. Findmypast (p.17) also offers free third party indexes to the NLI records platform, through its 'Ireland Roman Catholic Parish Baptisms', 'Ireland Roman Catholic Parish Marriages', and 'Ireland Roman Catholic Parish Burials' collections.

For records from the city of Dublin, and counties Kerry, Carlow and Cork (excluding Cork city), visit the free to consult IrishGenealogy platform at **www.irishgenealogy.ie**, or more specifically via **https://churchrecords.irishgenealogy.ie/churchrecords/**.

Transcripts of additional Catholic records can be accessed at the pay-per-view RootsIreland platform (p.20).

The Protestant Churches

For the Protestant churches there are a variety of sources to consult. The starting point for online access for the whole of Ireland is RootsIreland (p.20), although the holdings of Protestant denomination records for each county differ, depending on the priorities of the county centres creating the transcripts.

For free-to-access Church of Ireland records for Dublin city, as well as parishes in counties Kerry and Carlow, visit IrishGenealogy (**www.irishgenealogy.ie**).

Northern Ireland's national archive, PRONI (p.13), does not host church records online, but does offer a superb research guide called the PRONI Guide to Church Records, at **www.nidirect.gov.uk/publications/guide-church-records**. This details which denominational records are held at the facility for each parish in Ulster, as well as some cross-border areas, the years for which they are available, and whether the holdings are in microfilm format, digitised (for on-site access only), or the original registers. If records have not survived, this will be indicated, as will be the case if records are still held by the institution in questions.

Some additional Church of Ireland records have been indexed by the Representative Church Body Library in Dublin and made available online through the Anglican Record Project at **www.ireland.anglican.org/about/rcb-library/anglican-record-project**.

The Presbyterian Historical Society of Ireland (**https://presbyterianhistoryireland.com**) hosts additional records in Belfast.

Census Records

Census records provide a snapshot of family member at their homes on a regular basis, and thus can be very helpful to link family members together in one place and time. Beyond stating their names, they can also be very useful in providing additional information about them, such as their ages, religious denominations, abilities to read and write, their occupations and where they were born. Unfortunately, the survival of such censuses is not great when compared to Britain, despite Ireland being a part of the same United Kingdom at the time they were created.

Although the first modern Irish census was recorded in 1813, it was so poorly carried out that it was never officially presented to the UK

Parliament. It was not until 1821 that they got it right, after which a census was carried out every ten years until 1911. Sadly, very little has survived from the 1821–1851 censuses, and practically nothing from 1861 to 1891, with a combination of some records being pulped for paper in the First World War, and others destroyed during the Four Courts fire in 1922. This means that, with a few exceptions for some areas from 1821 to 1871, the only records to have survived are those from 1901 and 1911. No census was carried out in 1921 because of the War of Independence, and, following Partition, the last time a census was carried out on the same night in the North and the South was in 1926. Although there have been many censuses carried out in the Free State/Republic and Northern Ireland since then, all of these, including the 1926 records, are currently closed for access for one hundred years for privacy purposes. The 1926 records from the Free State will be released in 2026, but the equivalent records from the North have unfortunately not survived.

The surviving censuses from 1901 and 1911, as well as some surviving fragments from 1821 to 1851, are freely available to search via the National Archive of Ireland digital records platform at **https://nationalarchives.ie/collections/search-the-census/**

If your Irish ancestors migrated to Britain, there is a much better survival rate of records there from 1841 to 1921. Original records from England, Wales and the Channel Islands are available to consult on Ancestry, Findmypast, TheGenealogist, My Heritage, and FamilySearch (all of which are explored further later in this chapter). These sites also carry incomplete transcripts of records for Scotland, but for the original records themselves, with all the details recorded, visit ScotlandsPeople (**www.scotlandspeople.gov.uk**).

Wills

The last of the basic records that can help to get you started with your initial research are wills and testaments left by family members when they died. In such documents the deceased will have noted names of family members and friends to whom he or she wished to give various bequests, which can again be very helpful to connect various relatives together into respective family groups.

Again, the survival of such records is badly affected by the devastation unleashed on the Four Courts in 1922, however, there are surviving copies of some records prior to this, as well as records generated after the tragedy in the North and South.

The NAI hosts a Guide to Testamentary Records at **www.nationalarchives.ie/article/testamentary-record**, and among its digitised holdings at **www.genealogy.nationalarchives.ie** is a database entitled 'Prerogative and diocesan copies of some wills and indexes to others, 1596–1858'. This includes surviving indexes to wills which did not survive 1922, but also some copies of wills that have survived from the Prerogative Court (covering 1664–84, 1706–8, 1726–8, 1728–9, 1777, 1813 and 1834) and for the Diocesan Courts of Connor (1818–20, 1853–8) and Down (1850–8). There is also a 'Calendars of Wills and Administrations 1858–1920' on the site, offering summaries of cases taken through the probate courts, while events after this for the Republic can be accessed on the National Archives of Ireland's catalogue (p.13).

For Northern Ireland, many surviving pre-1858 indexes have been integrated into a free database called 'Name Search' on the PRONI website at **www.nidirect.gov.uk/information-and-services/search-archives-online/name-search**. If a surviving copy of the will exists and is held at PRONI, this is stated alongside the index entry. A calendar of wills from 1858 to 1965, confirmed in the Northern district probate offices (Belfast, Armagh, Londonderry), is available on the PRONI website; accompanying copies of wills may also be found in the earlier years through the database, available at **www.nidirect.gov.uk/information-and-services/search-archives-online/will-calendars**.

Many transcripts and abstracts of wills were also compiled by various folk prior to the Four Courts fire, and a useful guide summarising some of these is available on the FamilySearch website at **www.familysearch.org/wiki/en/Ireland_Probate_Records**, noting collections compiled by Sir William Betham, Sir John Bernard Burke, Wallace Clare, Rev. William Carrigan, Philip Crosslé and others. Some indexes and abridgements are hosted on sites such as Findmypast and Ancestry, which in most cases will note the names of those who left estate or who were granted administrative bonds. It may not be much, but they can at least help to confirm the period when an ancestor might have passed away.

The Registry of Deeds, Dublin: Abstracts of Wills (3 vols: 1708–45, 1746–85, 1785–1832), also notes many cases where wills were recorded within the Registry of Deeds, which can often contain useful information about property. Copies of these can be found in many libraries, but the Irish Manuscripts Commission website at **www.irishmanuscripts.ie** hosts free to access digitised editions, while Ancestry also offers a searchable database version of the first two volumes.

DNA Testing

The most unique genealogical record that we can use is our very own DNA. We inherit DNA from our parents, who inherited it from their parents before them, and so on. For every generation that we go back in our tree we will have distant cousins who share some of our genetic inheritance from common ancestors. By doing a test and uploading the results online with an attached family tree, we can look for these relatives, some of whom may just have inherited the family Bible, diaries and stories that our ancestors left behind.

The three main types of DNA tested for family history purposes are as follows:

i) Y-DNA is passed from a father to his sons, and as it is through such relationships that a family surname has historically been passed on to the next generation, it can be used to do surname studies going back centuries. By its very nature only men can be tested for Y-DNA, although women can ask a father, brother, grandfather, uncle or male cousin to be tested on their behalf.

ii) Mitochondrial DNA (mtDNA) is passed from a mother to her children. The mtDNA inherited by a mother comes from her mother, and her maternal grandmother before her, etc. While it can be tested, its use in genealogy tends to be more for specialised purposes. (Note that another form of DNA is usually tested alongside mtDNA, called X-chromosome DNA or X-DNA, but not all companies report on it; again, it is useful in limited circumstances.)

iii) Autosomal DNA is a type of DNA that we inherit roughly 50 per cent from each parent. From our grandparents this will then mean we will have inherited approximately 25 per cent of their DNA from each of them, and so on. This type of test is useful to try to determine close cousins within the last five to six generations, before the shared amounts from earlier generations become too small to make meaningful matches. This is by far the most commonly tested form of DNA, and can be used to make connections with distant cousins related to us through common ancestors shared over the last two centuries. As such, this is the test to perhaps start with.

Several commercial companies offer DNA tests for genealogical purposes, including FamilyTreeDNA (**www.familytreedna.com**), Ancestry (**www.ancestry.co.uk/dna**), and MyHeritage (**www.myheritage.com**). Not every company will offer tests for all types of DNA though, with both MyHeritage and Ancestry, for example, only testing for autosomal DNA.

In my book *Sharing Your Family History Online* (Pen and Sword, 2021) I provide a detailed beginner's guide to using DNA for research, while the North of Ireland Family History Society (p.25) also regularly runs a

> **CASE STUDY:** To give an example of how useful autosomal DNA can be for research, I recently broke a twenty-year-long brick wall concerning my three-times-great-grandmother, Teresa Mooney (1834–1919), from Dublin. I knew from records concerning her two marriages, in Corfu in 1862 and in Nenagh, Tipperary, in 1866, that her father was a weaver called Thomas Mooney, and that her mother was called Mary Ann. Teresa was buried in Glasnevin Cemetery in an unmarked grave, and with no other relatives in the same lair, it was impossible to find further information about her parents.
>
> However, thanks to a recent DNA match with a distant cousin in the United States, descended from a brother of Teresa's, also called Thomas, I was eventually able to flesh out her entire family. In addition to her brother Thomas, I discovered that Teresa also had two sisters, Mary and Esther, and that her father was Thomas Mooney (1805–1872), a weaver and later a news vendor, and her mother Mary Ann McCaul (1804–1899), both of whom were also buried at Glasnevin.

regular series of workshops. More detailed books on the topic include *The Family Tree Guide to DNA Testing and Genetic Genealogy* by Blaine Bettinger, and *Tracing Your Ancestors Using DNA: A Guide for Family Historians*, by Graham S. Holton, John Cleary, Michelle Leonard, Iain McDonald and Alasdair F. MacDonald.

> **TIP:** If you test with Ancestry you can export your DNA results from its website and then import them into the other DNA testing platforms. The advantage of doing this is that you will be able to massively expand the range of possible contacts that you might likely make.

Gateway Sites

There are many other Irish records that can be consulted online, as well as sites offering advice on aspects of research. Many 'gateway sites' can help to locate such records and platforms, but such is the rate of new material coming and old sites dying off and not being renewed that occasionally dead links can appear. If this happens, it is worth searching for the named collection on a search engine such as Google to see if it might be available in another format elsewhere, or by checking a digital archive such as the Internet Archive (**https://archive.org**).

Dublin based genealogist John Grenham's Irish Ancestors site (**www.johngrenham.com**) offers resources and tools which he previously created for the now defunct *Irish Times* site of the same name, some of which are free. His exceptionally useful 'Placenames' tab allows you to locate the parish of a particular place of interest and to view it on a map. The 'Browse' area is the real workhorse of the site, however, which allows for the identification of record collections which may exist for a particular area, including shelf marks for library holdings and archive held records, detailed lists of civil and Roman Catholic parish maps, and more. The 'Sitemap' page (**www.johngrenham.com/sitemap.php**) can readily take you to the area of interest without going through the menu based tabs. John's advice can also be consulted though his book *Tracing Your Irish Ancestors: 5th edition*, an essential for every genealogist's library.

Claire Santry's Irish Genealogy Toolkit at **www.irish-genealogy-toolkit.com** provides a handy introduction to some of the key record resources available for research in Ireland, North and South, as well as lists of useful contacts and downloadable free resources, such as charts and forms.

Jane Lyons' From Ireland at **www.from-ireland.net** offers a range of free resources, the result of a research effort first started in 1996. Many record sets are transcribed, while the site also contains thousands of photographs and inscriptions taken in graveyards across the island. The various collections are accessible by following the grey links on the 'Explore' bar in the middle of the screen.

For the province of Ulster, William Roulston's *Researching Ulster Ancestors: The Essential Genealogical Guide to Early Modern Ulster 1600–1800: 2nd edition* (Ulster Historical Foundation, 2018) is another essential for the library, detailing key records for each of the nine counties that can be accessed at PRONI and other repositories. (Overseas, the book is published as *Researching Scots-Irish Ancestors*.)

Irish Archives

There are several major archival institutions across the island of Ireland which host many valuable resources online, although at some stage you will probably need to visit the institutions directly as your research progresses.

The National Archives of Ireland (NAI) is the main national repository for the Republic of Ireland, which in recent years has been working with partner agencies to make some of its holdings accessible online, with many of these freely available at **https://genealogy.nationalarchives.**

ie. Digitised records from the archive can also be found on Findmypast (p.17) and FamilySearch (p.22).

The NAI's online catalogue is found on its main website at **www.nationalarchives.ie**, listing items predominantly generated by the Irish government and the courts, and acting as the gateway to some additional digitised records. The site's pages also include useful resource guides which are located under the 'Genealogy' tab at the top of the home page, while the 'Digital Resources' section of the site, accessible from the top menu, leads to a range of standalone web based projects.

The NAI is the successor to the earlier Public Record Office of Ireland in Dublin. A major project currently underway is the Virtual Records Treasury of Ireland, at **https://virtualtreasury.ie**, which not only provides an inventory of what was lost at the Four Courts fire in 1922 (and what has survived), but which has also digitally recreated a 3D virtual reality reconstruction of the destroyed Record Treasury building. The virtual building is populated with fully-searchable digital surrogates of surviving documents, as well as copies of lost records sourced from partner institutions across the world.

North of the border, the national archive is the Public Record Office of Northern Ireland (PRONI), based at Titanic Quarter in Belfast. Its

Established after the destruction of the PRO in 1922, PRONI is the national archive of Northern Ireland.

fairly comprehensive website at **www.nidirect.gov.uk/proni** (also **www.nidirect.gov.uk/campaigns/public-record-office-northern-ireland-proni**) offers free access to many digitised records databases, including the 1912 Ulster Covenant, maps, a wills database, and more.

Other valuable research resources include the archive's all important catalogue, and a series of information leaflets and guides to PRONI held records. These guides are available as downloadable PDF formatted documents, including the all important PRONI Guide to Church Records (p.7), and various others on additional topics such as newspapers that can be consulted at the facility, as well as privately deposited collections. The leaflets section contains a useful series of background documents on a further range of subjects including local history and emigration.

PRONI's eCatalogue contains detailed descriptions of records, some of them containing entire transcripts of letters and other resources, so it is always worth doing a name search for your relatives within it. The catalogue can be both searched and browsed.

To find collections within the island's city and county based archives you can visit the site of the repository itself, or utilise the Irish Archives Resource website at **https://iar.ie**, which provides an option to search for resources held in over forty repositories across Ireland. Direct links to the participants can be found at **https://iar.ie/public-private-archives-repositories-ireland/**.

The university sector offers many important resources, one of the most notable being The Dúchas Project (**www.duchas.ie**) from University College Dublin (UCD) and Fiontar agus Scoil na Gaeilge, Dublin City University (DCU). This features materials from the National Folklore Collection, including The Schools Collection, a wonderful collection of folklore compiled by schoolchildren in Ireland in the 1930s, and its Photographic Collection.

> **TIP:** Many archives will have records that are closed to public access to protect the privacy of people still alive, with such closure periods often in place for a hundred years. This may also apply to the closure of entire volumes which may contain earlier records. Records may also be inaccessible for conservation reasons. If unsure if a record is available, ask the relevant archivist.

British Archives

The whole of Ireland was integrated into the United Kingdom from 1801 to 1922, while Northern Ireland still is, meaning that many British repositories can be equally important for your research. The National Archives (TNA) is the main UK archive, predominantly carrying material from England and Wales. Its website at **www.nationalarchives.gov.uk** contains research and resources guides, as well as a phenomenal amount of digitised material, accessible through its 'Discovery' catalogue.

Among the archive's Irish holdings are resources specifically dedicated to the running of the country. These include administration records from Dublin Castle, service records for members of the Royal Irish Constabulary, and materials relevant to the Easter Rising of 1916 (p.142). The State Papers collections also detail the archives of the various Secretaries of State for Ireland from 1509 to 1782, an important collection which acts as a substitute for many pre-1790 Dublin Castle papers which were lost in 1922 during the destruction of the Public Record Office in the city.

Holdings for many British county based archives and other repositories are now included within TNA's Discovery catalogue. The site's Find an Archive page at **https://discovery.nationalarchives.gov.uk/find-an-archive** can also help with contact details and web links for specific archives.

The main national institution north of the border is the National Records of Scotland (**www.nrscotland.gov.uk**). The Your Scottish Archives website at **https://yourscottisharchives.com** and the Scottish Council on Archives at **www.scottisharchives.org.uk** can also help locate more local archive holdings, while Scottish collections in private hands can be found by consulting the National Register of Archives for Scotland catalogue at **https://catalogue.nrscotland.gov.uk/nrasregister/welcome.aspx**.

While Wales does not have its own dedicated national archive as such, the National Library of Wales (p.17) has many resources that can help.

> **TIP:** Ireland effectively has three main national archives – PRONI, the NAI and the UK National Archives. Try not to get into the mindset that records for the South should only be looked for at the NAI, and for the North at PRONI, because each archive holds records from across the island. The UK National Archive has further holdings for Irish folk in a British context.
>
> Check all three, every time!

Libraries

The home page of the website for the Dublin based National Library of Ireland (NLI) at **www.nli.ie** offers a 'Family History' research area via the main menu, with a great deal of advice for those planning a visit to the institution, including an introductory research guide.

The NLI site also provides access to its catalogue at **https://catalogue.nli.ie**, which includes electronically added records from 1990 onwards, with earlier handwritten entries continuing to be added. The 'Sources' database at **https://sources.nli.ie** also details over 180,000 catalogue records, comprising manuscripts and periodicals catalogued up to the 1980s, manuscripts held in other repositories in Ireland and overseas listed from the 1940s–70s, and materials from over 150 Irish periodicals catalogued up to 1969.

Many of the Republic's county based libraries have contributed e-books to the Ask About Ireland website at **www.askaboutireland.ie/reading-room/digital-book-collection/**.

A further useful repository in Dublin is the Oireachtas Library, accessible via **www.oireachtas.ie**, which services Dáil Éireann and Seanad Éireann. Its catalogue site at **https://opac.oireachtas.ie** also offers access to many digitised gems of value to the family historian.

The National Library of Ireland in Dublin.

There is no national library for Northern Ireland, but two key repositories are Belfast Central Library and the Linen Hall Library. The website for the former at **www.librariesni.org.uk/libraries/greater-belfast/belfast-central-library/** unfortunately provides little more than contact details and opening hours information. The main parent site at **www.librariesni.org.uk** provides contact information on local library branches across Northern Ireland.

The Linen Hall Library, initially founded in 1788 as the Belfast Reading Society, is the last remaining subscribing library in Ireland, and has a much more substantial presence online at **https://linenhall.com**. Under 'About Us', the 'Our Collections' category holds information about many holdings of the institution, including its 'Irish & Local Studies' section. Also available is an online catalogue, offering search options by keyword, title, author's name or journal title.

The British Library in London may offer further assistance at **www.bl.uk**, and the National Library of Scotland in Edinburgh at **www.nls.uk**. The National Library of Wales (Llyfrgell Genedlaethol Cymru), based in Swansea, acts as both a national library and a national archive for the Welsh, and is online at **www.library.wales**.

Commercial Vendors

Family history is a fairly competitive business for commercial vendors, offering a vast range of genealogically useful online materials either by subscription or on a pay-per-view basis.

When subscribing to sites, note that some offer an introductory period for free, which you will need to register for with your credit card details; do be aware of their terms and conditions for use. Also note that some vendors take credit card details when you register and at the end of the free period then 'automatically renew' your subscription. Check to see if there is a tick box that allows you to stop this from happening, or make sure you cancel your subscription before the renewal period approaches, if you do not wish for a lump sum to suddenly disappear from your bank account! It is also worth signing up to the newsletters and social media platforms of many of the sites, for news of free access periods to certain collections.

Findmypast
www.findmypast.co.uk
Findmypast originally started in the UK as **www.findmypast.co.uk**, offering indexes to civil registration records for English and Welsh births, marriages and deaths from 1837 onwards, and later expanding to

offer British census records and parish records. Today the site has several worldwide platforms, including Findmypast Ireland (**www.findmypast.ie**), Findmypast Australasia (**www.findmypast.com.au**) and the US based Findmypast (**www.findmypast.com**).

Findmypast's Irish venture was launched in 2011 as a partnership between Dublin based history and heritage company Eneclann and the Scottish based technology giant Brightsolid. The Irish team has facilitated access to various digitised records sourced by itself and in partnership with bodies such as the NAI. Although each worldwide Findmypast site started off with very different offerings, their records are now collectively accessible through each platform, by various subscription means. This means that while Irish records can be easily searched through all the platforms, it is also possible to search for Irish emigrants who made lives in overseas territories. The British offerings are especially useful, as many 'British' records include Irish citizens from the period when the Republic was within the UK.

Findmypast's holdings are arranged in the following categories:

- Birth, marriage, death and parish
- Churches and religion
- Education and work
- Travel and migration
- Newspapers & publications
- Military, armed forces and conflict
- Census, land and surveys
- Directories and social history
- Institutions and organisations
- 1939 Register

A global search facility across all collections is also available, along with an A–Z listing, and a separate facility to search the English and Welsh 1939 Register.

The following are just some of the Irish databases available through the site:

- Ireland, Petty Sessions Court Registers
- Ireland Dog Licence Registers
- Irish Prison Registers 1790–1924
- Griffith's Valuation 1847–1864
- Ireland, Belfast & Ulster Directories
- Ireland Valuation Office Books

- Dublin Workhouses Admission & Discharge Registers 1840–1919
- Ireland Calendars of Wills & Administrations 1858–1965 Ireland, Society of Friends (Quaker) Congregational Records
- Dublin Poor Law Unions Board of Guardians Minute Books
- Ireland, Royal Irish Constabulary Service Records 1816–1922
- Donegal Workhouses Registers and Minute Books
- Clare Poor Law Unions Board of Guardians Minute Books
- Galway Poor Law Union Records

Ancestry
www.ancestry.co.uk
Ancestry.co.uk is the UK platform for the American based Ancestry.com corporation, which, as with Findmypast, has various web domains offering access to its collections across the world. Although the Utah based company has international headquarters in Dublin, to deal with its non-US based material, there is no separately branded Irish domain for the website. The UK site does hold many Irish records on a dedicated subsection of its site at **www.ancestry.co.uk/cs/irish**, but the most complete listings of Irish collections is found within the site's 'Card Catalogue', or by using the 'Explore by Location' map function on the main 'Search' page (Northern Ireland is listed under the 'United Kingdom' section, and Ireland under 'Europe').

Among the most useful Irish resources are:

- Irish Civil Registration Birth, Marriage and Death Indexes (1845–1958)
- Births and Baptisms 1620–1911
- Roman Catholic parish records
- Various Irish newspapers, including *The Belfast News-Letter* 1738–1925
- Ireland and Northern Ireland, Newspapers.com Stories and Events Index, 1800s to current
- Land records, including Griffith's Valuation and Tithe Applotment books
- Records of the Scots-Irish
- Immigration and travel records
- Royal Irish Constabulary 1816–1921 records
- Photographic collections
- Londonderry, Northern Ireland, City Cemetery Burials, 1853–1961
- Scotland and Northern Ireland, Death Index, 1989–2023
- Ireland, Irish Emigration Lists, 1833–1839

In addition, Ancestry has several third party indexes for databases that appear on the PRONI website (p.14), which in some cases are superior to PRONI's own search tools. These include:

- Northern Ireland, Street Directories, 1819–1900
- Ireland, Wills and Admons, 1515–1858
- Northern Ireland, Valuation Revision Books, 1864–1933
- Ireland, Ulster, Census of Protestant Householders, 1740
- Web: Belfast, Northern Ireland, Burial Indexes, 1869–2011
- Web: Northern Ireland, Will Calendar Index, 1858–1965
- Web: Ulster, Ireland, Ulster Covenant, 1912
- Web: Northern Ireland, Freeholders Records, 1662–1839

As with Findmypast, there are many 'British' collections which include records for Irish based ancestors, particularly on the military front.

Ancestry also offers a free tree building facility, and its DNA platform at **www.ancestry.co.uk/dna** is one of the most powerful genealogical research tools available for tracing genetic cousins.

> **TIP:** Some commercial platforms temporarily offer free access to certain records collections at times of commemoration or remembrance, which may help you to save money. You can also sign up to a free trial with some platforms, where you will be asked to provide billing details as if you are taking out a paid subscription. Once you have signed up, immediately cancel your subscription, you should still have access for the rest of the trial period.

RootsIreland
www.rootsireland.ie
RootsIreland is the subscription-based online records platform of the Irish Family History Foundation (p.25). The site hosts the largest collection of transcribed Irish parish records online, as well as other collections, and covers most of the island, with records sourced from county based genealogy centres located in the North and the South.

The participating counties in the project can be identified by a map on the home page. The records available vary considerably between counties, however, dependant on which projects the respective genealogy centres have been working on. This means that while one county may only provide Roman Catholic records, its neighbour might well offer transcriptions of civil records, censuses and Anglican parish

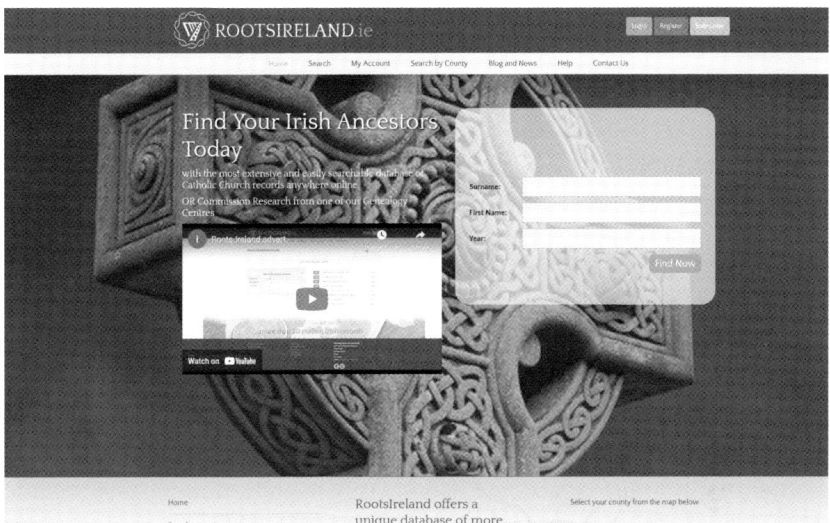

RootsIreland provides many useful transcripts of records from across Ireland.

records. A detailed guide on which records are offered county-by-county is included via the 'Online Sources' tool found under the 'Help' option of the main menu. Material is constantly added, so it is worth regularly returning to look for updates, and/or subscribing to its newsletter.

You need to register for access, after which you can then perform an all-Ireland based search, or a more targeted search for a particular county. This can be done by selecting the area of interest using the interactive map on the home page or via the 'Search by County' option on the main menu at the top.

Once you have keyed in the search criteria and hit return, you will be told how many matches have been found. To access the transcripts you will need to purchase a subscription, with options available for one day (twenty-four hours), a month, six months, or a year.

Many of the areas which do not participate on RootsIreland instead have records freely hosted on another site, IrishGenealogy (p.4), which is an Irish government sponsored venture.

TheGenealogist
www.thegenealogist.co.uk

TheGenealogist website does not have much by way of Irish holdings, but does carry the records of the mid-nineteenth century land valuation known as Griffith's Valuation, which can act as a census substitute, as well as a few trade directories and land records. In addition, the site has started to offer some Roman Catholic parish records collections, including material for counties Tipperary, Laois, Kildare, Wexford and Carlow.

MyHeritage
www.myheritage.com
There is not a great deal of unique Irish material on MyHeritage, but it does have some surprises, including databases such as 'Irish Prisoners 1780–1867', various county directories from across the island, and the original Irish GRO indexes to the civil registration records of births, marriages and deaths. Its DNA platform is a further important tool.

FamilySearch
www.familysearch.org
The online presence of the Church of Jesus Christ of Latter-day Saints, whose members have a theological requirement to research their ancestors. Records are free to access via standalone databases and through its catalogue facility. Local family history centres worldwide can also provide further records access (**https://locations.familysearch.org/en**).

Newspapers

Newspapers are perhaps the most important records that can help the family historian beyond the basic genealogy records, because they can actually tell us stories about what they once got up to, as well as provide us with a contemporary context to the daily lives that they led. They can be particularly important to plug gaps with the vital records through announcements and intimations, as well as to provide coverage of trials and other circumstances for which the original documentary records may not have survived, particularly for cases involving the courts for which very little survived the Four Courts fire in 1922.

A fairly substantial collection of published newspapers, as well as a comprehensive listing of newspaper content known to have been printed in Ireland, is available at the National Library of Ireland, with a dedicated guide to the records available at **www.nli.ie/collections/our-collections/newspapers**. As well as holdings from the Joly Collection, and content sourced from the Royal Dublin Society Library, the NLI also partnered with the British Library between the 1980s and the early part of the twenty-first century on the NEWSPLAN project (and its successor, NEWSPLAN 2000), to catalogue and make available on microfilm a range of titles from across the island of Ireland. The project's report for Ireland can be accessed through the NLI catalogue at **https://catalogue.nli.ie/Record/vtls000042992**.

Belfast Newspaper Library is located within the city's Central Library.

In Belfast, the Newspaper Library at Belfast Central Library (**www.librariesni.org.uk/resources/cultural-heritage/newspaper-library**), holds the largest collection of titles for Northern Ireland. The site's website provides a detailed list of all holdings available on microfilm, although there is a stated caveat with the coverage range for each title, in that there may be gaps within the broad ranges cited. In addition to the microfilms at the Newspaper Library are various hard-copy holdings, although a catalogue listing for these is not available online. A list of titles has been collated in-house and can be consulted on a visit, but the library is happy for users to contact it in advance of a visit to see if a desired title is held there.

The subscription-based British Newspaper Archive (BNA) at **www.britishnewspaperarchive.co.uk** is a joint venture between the British Library (**www.bl.uk**), which has a dedicated newspaper library base at Boston Spa, Yorkshire, and the records platform Findmypast (p.17). The content on the site can be equally accessed as part of a subscription on Findmypast. Also available online is the subscription-based Irish Newspaper Archives (INA) at **www.irishnewsarchive.com**, which carries additional titles not located on the BNA (and in some cases, different coverage ranges for material that is), making both platforms equally essential for Irish research.

The *Belfast Gazette* commenced publication from 7 June 1921 as the official newspaper of state for Northern Ireland, with all titles freely available at **www.thegazette.co.uk**. The paper carries a range of reports on military events, honours and promotions, the awarding of civil honours, business announcements (such as partnerships agreements and bankruptcies), land sales announcements, probate notices, parliamentary bills gaining Royal Assent, and considerably more. As well as the site's own search tools, Findmypast hosts a 'Ireland, *Belfast Gazette* 1922–2018' database.

Prior to Partition, the all Ireland *Dublin Gazette* did the same job, commencing its run in 1706. There is no single collection of this title online, but the largest available collection covers the period from 1750 to 1800, and is freely available from the Irish Parliament's Oireachtas Library website at **https://opac.oireachtas.ie**. Findmypast also offers a database providing access to this collection, entitled 'Ireland, *Dublin Gazette* 1750–1800'. For post-1921 check **www.irisoifigiuil.ie**.

The following search tips may help for newspaper research:

i) If newspapers are available on microfilm, but have been digitised by either the BNA or the INA, you can carry out free online searches, and note down any finds for consultation on the microfilms later.

ii) When carrying out searches for people, note the context in which you are trying to seek them. For example, a death notice may well be printed as 'Prendergast, Maurice', rather than 'Maurice Prendergast'.

iii) Try to construct searches on terms just beyond names – for example:
- 'Maurice Prendergast' +'31 New Street'
- 'Prendergast' +'New Street'
- '31 New Street'

iv) Remember that there may have been more than one edition of a title produced in a single day; microfilms and digitised copies tend to feature one edition only.

v) Newspapers that have been bound prior to being microfilmed or digitised may present problems, as pages that curve in towards the spine can be distorted when photographed. This can lead to problems when searching on databases, as the software used to create the searchable text from the image (known as 'optical character recognition', or 'OCR'), may be unable to read the article in question. Sometimes it pays to browse through a title rather than to simply rely on keyword searching.

Societies

There are several genealogical and historical societies in Ireland, with many offering online holdings and listings. On the genealogical front the island is fairly fragmented, with various independent societies falling under different organisational bodies.

The Council of Irish Genealogical Organisations (**www.cigo.ie**) is an umbrella body which has several groups among its membership, the details for which can be accessed in the 'Constituent Organisations' page. The most useful part of its website for non-members is the 'Links' page, as this provides a fairly detailed list of agencies and records categories covering everything from 'Adoption' to 'Workhouses', as well as a handy list of county archive websites within the Republic.

The Irish Family History Foundation is the cross-border coordinating body for several county based genealogy centres across Ireland, which hosts the RootsIreland platform (p.20). The website also offers contact details for the centres, which can offer research assistance.

Established in 1990, the Genealogical Society of Ireland has a dedicated research and archive centre, An Daonchartlann, based at Carlisle Pier in Dún Laoghaire. Its website at **www.familyhistory.ie** hosts indexes to its journals from 1992 as well as its monthly *Ireland's Genealogical Gazette* from 2006, the latter being freely available to read online. The society is also on YouTube at **www.youtube.com/channel/UCGqe3_Od9gfksqocu3YuywQ**.

Based in Kent, England, the Irish Genealogical Research Society (**www.irishancestors.ie**) was formed in 1936 with a remit to locate and collate copies of records that had been destroyed at the Public Record Office of Ireland in Dublin during the Civil War. The society publishes an annual journal called *The Irish Genealogist*, and its website hosts many unique database resources, some of them freely accessible.

The North of Ireland Family History Society (**www.nifhs.org**) is the umbrella body for family history societies in Northern Ireland, with branches based in Ballymena, Belfast, Causeway, Foyle, Killyleagh, Larne, Lisburn, Newtownabbey, North Armagh, South Tyrone and Tyrone. The site's Resources section offers a comprehensive overview of many of its Newtownabbey based research centre resources, as well as online offerings, including free to download forms for use when transcribing records. The society also provides additional services to its members, such as a look up facility for records at **www.nifhs.org/resources/look-up-service**, as well as a bi-annual journal called *North Irish Roots*.

There are two main umbrella groups for local studies societies, being the Federation for Ulster Local Studies Limited at **www.fuls.org.uk** and the Federation of Local History Societies (Conascadh na gCumann Staire Áitiúla) at **www.localhistory.ie**. Each website links to member sites across Ireland, providing a great deal of useful resources for historical research.

Commercial Research Services

If stuck on a research problem, professional genealogists might be able to assist. There are several professional bodies to which they might be a member, including the following:

- Association of Professional Genealogists
  www.apgen.org
- Accredited Genealogists Ireland
  https://accreditedgenealogists.ie
- Society of Genealogists of Northern Ireland
  www.sgni.net

Note that many family history societies across the island also offer research assistance, as do Irish Family History Foundation affiliated research centres – contact details for these can be found through the respective county pages on the RootsIreland website (p.20).

The Irish Family History Centre (**www.irishfamilyhistorycentre.com**) is located in the CHQ Building on Dublin's Custom House Quay, and is part of the EPIC The Irish Emigration Museum experience (**https://epicchq.com**). The centre was established by leading genealogy services

EPIC The Irish Emigration Museum, Dublin.

provider Eneclann (one of the partners behind Findmypast Ireland), and offers both a visitor centre, and dedicated research services.

The Ulster Historical Foundation (**https://ulsterhistoricalfoundation.com**), formed in 1956, has a research centre in Belfast and offers professional consultations and research services, as well as a document retrieval service from key archival repositories in Belfast. The foundation also has a considerably well developed online presence, with its website offering a range of transcribed records on a subscription or pay-per-view basis, and with various video tutorials to help get the best out of its resources. The organisation also offers a range of publications for purchase, with some available as e-books.

Chapter 2

FAMILY EVENTS AND RELATIONSHIPS

For many of our ancestors within Ireland, the most immediate pressures were those experienced within the family, the most influential and yet the most unofficial administrative unit of daily life. Every family had its own moral code and rules which usually adhered to those of the society around them and the state which governed them. Whenever a relative deviated from what was expected of them, not only could this cause problems within the family itself, it could also lead to its ostracisation as a unit within the local community. As a consequence, family members were expected to adhere to the laws of the household, and to confirm to the social norms of the time. When they failed to do so, attempts may have been made to hide any indiscretions in the hope that it would not be discovered; at the other extreme, a relative's welfare may have been sacrificed, or the individual cut off and abandoned in a bid to retain the family's own standing within society.

Ireland's record in encouraging, and in some cases facilitating, such a culture has not always been an honourable one from a modern day perspective, with both states, North and South, apologising in recent years for the excesses of certain institutions, and with inquiries still ongoing to this day to seek redress. Following Partition in particular, the two divided nations tried too hard to be an idea of what they should be after the removal of the other, without realising that they were still two sides of the same coin.

In this chapter I will look at some of the key events and situations of family life from which domestic scandals and hardships could emerge.

Births and Illegitimacy

Historically in Ireland, a child was expected to be born to married parents. If born 'out of wedlock', it was rendered as 'illegitimate' in the eyes of the church, the state, and throughout society, irrespective of whichever religious community he or she came from. The word was a harsh judgment imposed on the new arrival not by its mother, but by the church and state into which it was born; by definition it meant that the child was not deemed to be 'legitimate', thus denying it certain rights in life that those born to a married couple could enjoy. For much of the country's history the level of such children born as 'bastards' was low, but for those so labelled it could remain a stigma throughout their lives.

Upon discovery of her condition, the mother of an illegitimate child in Ireland could find herself abandoned by her family, such was the perceived dishonour caused to it, or find herself instantly dismissed from domestic service, particularly if the child's father was a member of the household being served. A young unmarried mother could find it almost impossible to marry any person other than the father of her child, assuming he was interested and willing to admit to his paternal responsibilities.

In some cases, a subsequent union could be loveless. In the *First Report of Commissioners for Inquiring into the Condition of the Poorer Classes in Ireland*, published for the UK Parliament in 1835, a report from the County Kildare parish of Cadamstown heard from the local Anglican minister, Rev. Mr Flanagan, that:

> in the six parishes under his care, with a population of 5,000, there is not on an average more than one bastard born every year. If the parents are known, the parish does not support them. The mothers sometimes desert, but in rare instances destroy the children. The fathers often neglect the children; a feeling of honour has frequently induced them to marry the mother.

(Anon (1835) *The First Report from His Majesty's Commissioners for Inquiring into the Condition of the Poorer Classes in Ireland*. Appendix (A) p.62. **https://archive.org/details/op1245191–1001/page/n77/**: accessed 30 October 2024)

The investigating panel was also informed by witnesses about the attitude of men towards unmarried mothers within the parish:

> A young man of the lowest class would feel degraded by marrying a woman who had had an illegitimate child by another. James Marks says, 'No Irishman would demean himself by such an act'. Girls who have had bastards seldom can get anyone to marry them except those men by whom they were seduced; they are looked on as degraded persons, and scarcely associated with. James Marks says, they, 'are generally looked down upon'. Bastards are looked on in the same view; a small farmer would refuse a match with a bastard. (Ibid.)

Ostracisation of young mothers by their families and their local communities could sometimes lead to much more desperate methods to try to provide for themselves and their child:

> Women are obliged to beg if wages are not granted, and they always beg at a distance from home; they may return when they think their misconduct forgotten. The children generally become vagrants, and their mothers are sometimes driven to prostitution. The refusal of the father to support the child often leads to great disputes, and sometimes to serious outrages. The necessity of begging often injures the health both of the mother and the child. (Ibid.)

In some cases drastic measures were taken by young pregnant women to avoid such an apparent shame, both for themselves and a perceived future life of hardship for their child. Infanticide was one solution employed by desperate mothers to avoid a life of stigma, one which led the Irish Parliament in October 1707 to enact a statute 'To prevent the destroying and murdering of bastard children'. The creation of foundling hospitals in the early eighteenth century was a further attempt to prevent such early deaths (p.43).

In recent generations, young pregnant women might disappear for a short period and return after delivering their child as if nothing had happened, with many migrating over the Irish Sea to Britain to give birth. In some cases the child remained within the family, with the status of a child born to the young teenage mother hidden; it is not uncommon to find instances in the surviving censuses of a child noted as the grandparents' daughter or son, rather than as their grandchild. In other circumstances the young mother may have fled to Britain to a mother and baby home, and after the birth then given the child up for adoption; such homes also operated in Ireland (p.40), and may equally have been employed.

CASE STUDY: My great-great-grandparents, George Morrow and Jane Mitchell, from the parish of Magheraculmoney in County Fermanagh, moved to Glasgow, Scotland, in the latter part of the nineteenth century. In the 1891 census they were noted as having three children, James, aged 26, Elizabeth (my great-grandmother), aged 21, and a daughter Ellen, aged 16, all said to have been born in Ireland. In researching the children, however, I could only find one birth entry for an Ellen Morrow in County Fermanagh between 1874 and 1876, who was noted as the daughter of a woman called Fanny Morrow, born on 19 July 1875 at Clonelly in County Fermanagh. The birth was subsequently registered by a Jane Morrow, and there was no name recorded for her father. This Ellen was baptised within the week at Tubride Church, Kesh, on 25 July 1875, with the baptismal record noting her father to be a Charles Gilmore.

It took many years to uncover the truth of the situation, but thanks to several DNA connections on both the Morrow and Mitchell lines, I was eventually able to work out that Ellen was indeed the granddaughter of George and Jane, with my great-great-grandmother the likely informant at her birth in 1875. 'Fanny Morrow' was Frances Morrow, born on 10 August 1857, who emigrated to the United States in 1875, shortly after she had given birth to Ellen, who was left behind for her parents to raise. In the States, Frances married to a John William Morris in Pulaski County, Indiana, just two years later in 1877, with whom she raised a family.

It is unknown if Ellen's true parental status was ever revealed to her (her parents' names do not appear on her Scottish death certificate, which would normally record such details), but she never married, eventually passing away in Scotland in 1947.

Abortion was another alternative. As this was only legalised in the Republic of Ireland in 2018 and in Northern Ireland in 2019, many women historically travelled to Britain for a termination of their pregnancy.

Many mothers with illegitimate children were forced to enter the workhouse to give birth and/or to gain financial support for their children, putting immense pressure on the system, although the numbers doing so from the 1860s began to decline. The 1862 Poor Law Amendment Act gave power to boards of guardians to reclaim the costs of maintaining an illegitimate child under the age of 14 from its putative father. For this to happen, the mothers were required to attend the petty sessions to swear on oath before a justice of the peace (p.82) as to the

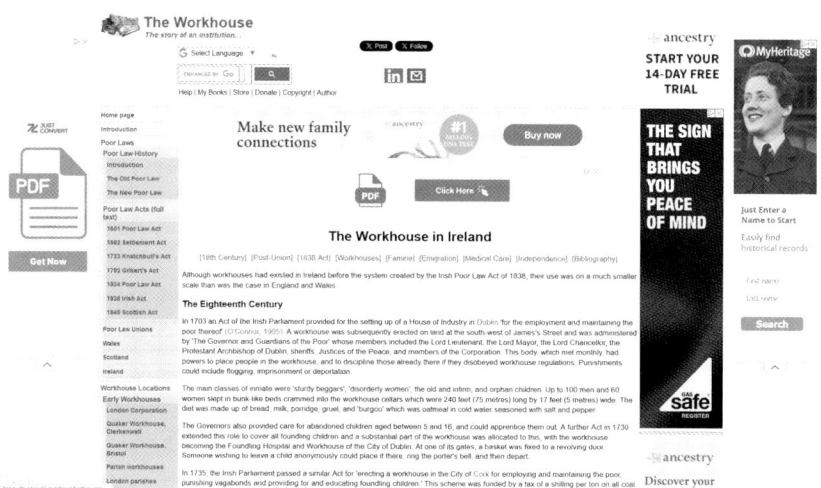

Peter Higginbotham's Workhouses.org website includes details of former institutions across Ireland.

identity of the child's father. Details of surviving workhouse records in Ireland can be found via Peter Higginbotham's **www.workhouses.org.uk**. Other institutions that sought to deal with unmarried mothers are dealt with from p.34.

The civil registration of births in Ireland was commenced by the state in 1864, some twenty-seven years after it had started in England and Wales, and nine years after it commenced in Scotland. Within a standard birth certificate many basic details were to be recorded, such as the name of the child, the date of birth and birthplace, the names of the parents, and the father's occupation. However, the initial 1863 Act for the Registration of Births and Deaths in Ireland did not state how illegitimate children should be recorded. It was not until a revising act of 1874 was passed that guidance was subsequently issued that stated:

> In the case of an illegitimate child no person shall, as father of such child, be required to give information under this Act concerning the birth of such child, and the registrar shall not enter in the registrar the name of any person as father of such child, unless at the joint request of the mother and of the person acknowledging himself to be the father of such child, and such person shall in such case sign the register, together with the mother.

As such, in many cases, the name of the father may be omitted from the civil record, but may be yet noted in a parallel church baptismal record.

> **CASE STUDY:** The first child of my wife's great-grandparents, Henry Giles and Johanna Donovan, was born illegitimately in Carrick-on-Suir, County Tipperary. The birth record noted him to be named 'Henry Donovan', born on 4 July 1870 in the town's Oven Lane, and with his mother as Johanna Donovan, but there was no mention of his father in the record.
>
> Young Henry was subsequently baptised at St Nicholas Roman Catholic Chapel on Saturday, 9 July 1870. In the baptismal record he was noted in Latin as 'Henricus Giles', the son of Henricus Giles and Johanna Giles, formerly Donovan. Tragically, just a day later, baby Henry died from convulsions, with his death record noting him again as 'Henry Giles'. However, it would not be until 24 July 1870 that Henry and Johanna actually married in Carrick-on-Suir.

The passing of the 1928 Legitimacy Act in Northern Ireland (**www.legislation.gov.uk/apni/1928/5/contents**) allowed for a child to be retrospectively legitimised if its parents had subsequently married, so long as they had been free to marry when the child was conceived, i.e. that the child was not born from an adulterous relationship. A similar provision was enacted by the Irish Free State in its Legitimacy Act of 1931 (**www.irishstatutebook.ie/eli/1931/act/13/enacted/en/print.html**), with further later revisions passed and enacted in both territories.

The actual status of 'illegitimacy' was not removed in the Republic until the 1987 Status of Children Act (**www.irishstatutebook.ie/eli/1987/act/26/enacted/en/print.html**), finally giving all children in the country the same rights, whether they had been born within or outside of a marriage.

> **TIP:** Surviving church records will commonly note the status of children baptised by the clergy. In Roman Catholic Church baptismal records a child might be stated as '*illegitimus*' in Latin, or '*ex illegitimo thoro*' (of illegitimate birth), whereas in the Protestant denominations he or she might be noted as 'illegitimate', 'natural born' or a 'bastard'.
>
> While a pregnant mother could not hide her situation in her community, an accused father could easily deny paternity, and in the Presbyterian and Anglican communities, kirk session records and vestry minutes could note investigations into such cases. Many of these records can be consulted at PRONI in Belfast or at the Dublin based Representative Church Body Library.

'Fallen Women'
There were other institutions which intervened to assist young unmarried mothers, or to which they were committed by their families or by the state. Charitable bodies such as the Catholic Rotunda Girl's Aid Society (founded 1880) and the Protestant based Dublin Hospital Girls Aid Association (1881) were also established, providing opportunities for work, although those given work were required to pay for services such as the nursing of their children, with a failure to do so seeing such mothers soon returned to the workhouse.

However, within Ireland another form of institution emerged which devastated the lives of many generations of women, and for which in recent years the Irish state has formally apologised, namely the Magdalene asylums or laundries. Described by Taoiseach Enda Kenny in 2013 as 'the nation's shame', these institutions, named for the biblical Mary Magdalene, provided a system of institutionalised control for what Ireland referred to as 'fallen women', dating back to the eighteenth century. The initial definition of a 'fallen woman' was a person who was engaged in prostitution, but the term was expanded across time to embrace any woman considered to have a moral deficiency; this included unmarried mothers, the daughters of unmarried mothers (many of them of school age), sexual abuse and rape victims, girls deemed to be flirtatious, as well as women committing minor crimes or suffering from mental health issues. All were incarcerated as 'penitent females'. Many were referred to the Magdalene laundries and asylums by judicial authorities, but some were sent to such institutions by their own parents, fearful of the judgement of wider society to them over their daughters' actions.

Despite such Magdalene laundries being predominantly run by Roman Catholic orders, the first institutions in Ireland were in fact established as asylums by the Protestant based Church of Ireland, following the creation of the Magdalene Hospital for the Reception of Penitent Prostitutes in London's Whitechapel in 1758. The Dublin Magdalene Asylum was established in 1765 on Gleeson Street, with a similar remit to bring poor Protestant women out of prostitution, until it eventually became a baby home in 1918. A further similar institution was set up by the church in Cork in 1810 as the Magdalene Asylum of Cork, and at Donegall Pass in Belfast from 1839, as the Ulster Magdalene Asylum. Further such premises were established in Britain, Australia and Canada, as well as within the United States.

Although the Anglican-run laundries and asylums had been joined by a small number of Presbyterian institutions on similar lines, following

Emancipation in 1829 it was under the auspices of the newly emboldened Roman Catholic movement that most of Ireland's future inmates would become punished. By the aftermath of the Famine (1845–1851), the majority of Ireland's Magdalene laundries were run by four orders, the Sisters of Mercy, the Sisters of Charity, the Sisters of Our Lady of Charity of Refuge, and the Good Shepherd Sisters, with their members widely admired by the establishment as the saviours of the 'impure'. The movement gained the favour of the Irish Parliamentary Party, which successfully campaigned from 1895 at the House of Commons in London for their laundries to be exempted from legislative controls.

An article in the *Freeman's Journal* from Wednesday, 18 July 1900, in which the authorities of the Magdalene Asylum at Galway made a public appeal for funds to alleviate a debt of £3,000 incurred by the construction of a new laundry, described the institution's work as follows, from its own perspective:

> There is no charity that appeals to the heart more strongly than to rescue the poor fallen woman. No other work will bring a greater blessing. To lift up the sinner from misery and shame – nameless degradation – is charity in the most touching and sublime form, and is particularly dear to the Saviour, Who made it His own special mission 'to seek and save that which was lost'.
>
> Without a home of this kind very little hope can be entertained for the reformation of this class. Cast off by parents, disowned by friends, branded as outcasts by the world, and maddened with the thought of what they were and what they might have been, they go on reckless and despairing from depths to deeper depths of sin, their lives a very foretaste of the hell to come.
>
> The Magdalene Asylum is then their only refuge and the only house that will receive them. Whenever God's grace speaks to their hearts its doors are always open to welcome them, and there they will be treated as though they had never fallen, and nothing left undone to bring comfort to their broken hearts. Thus the young who never fell perhaps but once, is saved from further contamination, and thus also the more hardened and confirmed are matched from those tempters of hell – who take advantage of their hungry and forlorn condition.
>
> And once within the Institution what a change! A life of useful labour and penance for the past – a life of contentment which they never found in sin – a life of prayer for those who helped to deliver them from temptation, and a life of gratitude to the good Lord for

all his Mercy. Thus the old life with all its misery and sin has passed away, and through God's grace they are no longer their former selves.

(*Freeman's Journal* (1900). Magdalene Asylum, Galway. Wednesday, 18 July. p.4. **www.britishnewspaperarchive.co.uk**: accessed 30 October 2024)

Following the Partition of Ireland, a monopoly of moral control over people's lives was maintained by the newly emergent southern state and the Catholic establishment, with any complaints against the harshness of the Magdalene system ignored and swept under a carpet. Despite the subsequent reformation of employment law, very few inspections took place within the laundries, permitting the exploitation of the women within them to continue.

While many women were released from service in an institution after a period of such 'penance', some remained trapped within the system throughout their entire lives, out of sight from society, and exploited as free labour in harsh, monastic settings, overseen by nuns as wardens. It was not just 'fallen women' who were sent to the laundries, however; mentally ill women and others who had been unable to cope after an institutionalised life within the orphanages and workhouses were also sent to do 'penance'. Women were often treated harshly in such institutions, being beaten and referred to by numbers, or simply as 'child', rather than the use of their names. Some women escaped, only to be returned by the local police officers, while those who were officially released received no financial support upon re-entering society.

The Magdalene laundries were as feared as the workhouse system by communities for over two centuries. However, it was not until the sale of land in 1993 at the former laundry site at High Park, Drumcondra, run by the Sisters of Our Lady of Charity, that the true horror of such institutions finally came to light. A mass grave containing 155 women was discovered, of whom only 75 had registered death certificates (similar mass burials have also been found at former Magdalene institutions at Glasnevin in Dublin, St Lawrence's in Limerick, and at Bohermore in Galway). All were cremated, but the resultant scandal opened up to the world the scale and trauma of the laundry system, eventually leading to the Irish government's 'Inter-Departmental Committee to Establish the Facts of State Involvement with the Magdalen Laundries' (**www.gov.ie/en/collection/a69a14–report-of-the-inter-departmental-committee-to-establish-the-facts-of/**), and the Taoiseach's state apology in 2013. The

> **CASE STUDY:** The *Meath Herald and Cavan Advertiser* from Saturday, 10 April 1926, reported that a 22-year-old woman named Bridget Lennon from Inishkeen, Co. Monaghan, had abandoned her baby daughter as a foundling at St Peter's Church, in Drogheda's West Street. She was arrested and conveyed to Mountjoy Prison, following an appearance at Drogheda District Court.
>
> The same paper followed up the story on Saturday, 22 May 1926, with Bridget having been once again brought before Drogheda District Court. She was accused of 'having broken her recognizances and absconded from the Magdalene Home, Dublin', as well as a charge of having 'deserted her infant child, aged one month, and rendered it liable to exposure, injury and bodily harm'.
>
> Upon being asked to plead, Lennon informed the justice that she had been told by a nun to clear out of the institution, a plea that the judge refused to accept. A police officer by the name of Sergeant Colville informed the judge that the young woman had become 'tired of being in the institution and ran away, and that a man followed her and brought her back'. A Superintendent O'Boyle then commented that the authorities had written to both the parish priest at Inishkeen, and Lennon's father, neither of whom had responded to him, and commented that she seemed a bit 'troublesome' to him.
>
> After being told that Lennon was 'not very strong in mind', but that she was not insane, the judge indicated that she would have to be sent to Mountjoy Prison, refusing to believe her again when she repeated that the nun at the asylum had told her that she had to leave. He informed her that 'She would have had a good home in the Magdalene Asylum if she had stayed in it,' to which Bridget responded that the girls in the prison had told her not to go back.
>
> To this he responded, 'But you will have to go back now, and for a month. I think it extraordinary that your parents did not take some interest in you. I hope that when the month is up that they will. It will be a very reprehensible thing if your parents don't look after you. It seems that the Sisters in the Magdalene Asylum were not able to do anything with you.'

payment of compensation to hundreds of surviving inmates has since followed.

It is estimated that more than 10,000 women were trapped within the system in the nineteenth century, with the numbers from the twentieth century simply unknown, the religious orders involved continuing to refuse to provide access to the relevant registers for those based within the institutions after 1900. From 1922 onwards, following Partition, ten laundries operated in Waterford, Cork, New Ross, Galway, Limerick and Dublin, with the last to close being at Sean McDermott Street (previously Gloucester Street) in Dublin, in 1996. Among the state and corporate clients using the laundry services provided by the institutions were the Irish Army, Guinness, the Bank of Ireland, and Áras an Uachtaráin, the Irish president's official residence.

In 2022, the Irish government announced that the former Magdalene laundry premises at Dublin's Sean McDermott Street would be converted into a National Centre for Research and Remembrance (**www.gov.ie/en/campaigns/0319a-national-centre-for-research-and-remembrance/**), although at the time of writing controversy continues with regards to access to records for those who spent time in such institutions. According to the government's website, the new centre 'will stand as a site of conscience to honour equally all those who spent time in Industrial Schools, Magdalene Laundries, Mother and Baby and County Home Institutions, Reformatories, and related institutions'.

The separate Justice for Magdalenes research platform (**http://jfmresearch.com**) offers a host of useful resources for those interested in learning more about the subject, including a Magdalene Oral History Project and Magdalene Names Project, as well as information concerning the Mother and Baby Homes Commission. The campaign's publication, *Ireland and the Magdalene Laundries: A Campaign for Justice* (IB Tauris/Bloomsbury, 2021) outlines the long journey to uncover the state's shame in perpetuating the system for so long.

In Northern Ireland, a similar institution continued to run in Belfast until 1977. At the time of writing, PRONI is identifying and preserving records for the Northern Irish Government's Truth Recovery Programme (**https://truthrecoverystrategy.com**), which is investigating the work of Magdalene Laundries, mother and baby homes (p.40) and workhouses (p.103), covering the period from 1922–95. Those wishing to contribute to the effort are invited to send submissions to the PRONI Truth Recovery Records team via **access@communities-ni.gov.uk** if you have, or are aware of, any historical documentary material that you think could be of interest. Those affected by such institutions are also advised to contact the Victims and Survivors Service (VSS) via 028 9031 1678 or by email at **support@vssni.org**.

You can also read more about Magdalene institutions across Ireland and Britain via Peter Higginbotham's Children's Homes site at **www.childrenshomes.org.uk**.

The former Magdalene laundry on Sean McDermott Street, Dublin, run by the Sisters of Our Lady of Charity, was the last to close in Ireland in 1996. It is to become a National Centre for Research and Remembrance.

Mother and Baby Homes

In addition to the Magdalene system, 'mother and baby homes' were also set up in Ireland to deal with what the establishment viewed as the 'problem' of unmarried mothers. Prior to 1921 there were only three such institutions in Ireland – at the Magdalene Asylum at Denny House, Dublin, established in 1765; at Pelletstown, on Navan Road, Dublin, established in 1904 (at premises which had earlier acted as a workhouse); and at Middle Abbey Street, Dublin, established by St Patrick's Guild in 1914 (replaced by premises at 39 Mountjoy Square in 1920). This expanded to eighteen homes after Partition. A list is available on Peter Higginbotham's site at **www.childrenshomes.org.uk/list/MB16.shtml**.

Pregnant girls as young as 12 were brought to the homes to be supported through their pregnancy and to give birth. Once the children were born they were separated from their mothers, and when old enough, were sent to boarding schools or reformatory schools. Their mothers were required to work for a period at the homes to repay the charity shown to them; some were sent subsequently to the Magdalene institutions, particularly those who had been to a home on more than one occasion. When mothers left the homes, they were required to contribute financially towards the upkeep of the children left behind, even though they had no right of access or custody.

The St Gerard's mother and baby home at 39 Mountjoy Square in Dublin, run by St Patrick's Guild, existed from 1920 to 1939.

In a 2013 report published by members of Adoption Rights Now, the following description was given of the punitive regime endured by those at a mother and baby home, later St. Peter's Hospital, at Castlepollard:

> Saint Peter's served as a Mother & Baby Home, a maternity hospital for single mothers, for thirty five years. Expectant mothers nearly always arrived at Castlepollard accompanied by their mothers and carrying a letter of reference from their local parish priest. Girls were stripped of their names and clothes as soon as their mothers left; their hair was clipped short, they were given rough uniforms and heavy wooden shoes/clogs, and assigned a 'house name'. They were ordered not to talk to each other.
>
> The sisters arrived to wake the girls before dawn every day and they would begin the daily routine of prayers and rosaries which carried on almost all day until bedtime. After a quick wash in cold water, their days began with a daily mass where priests preached fire and brimstone sermons alongside dire and graphic warnings of the eternal hellfire which awaited those would not abase and humiliate themselves before the might of the church and repent of their sins. Pride and vanity were the enemy. Temptation. Lust. Sins of the flesh. The seven deadly sins. Mortal sins. Endless lectures from sisters and the priest reminded the inmates of their 'sins'. Many were victims of rape and incest. Some were Priests' housekeepers who were there because of their Priests' behaviour. Pregnant girls often fainted during mass and were punished for their 'insolence' and 'disrespect'. Denied even the comfort of each others friendship and companionship during the day, the girls worked in silence or to the sound of prayers being endlessly repeated by the sisters. They were consistently underfed and almost universally refused even the most basic levels of healthcare and medical attention. They were not allowed to wear bras to protect their sensitive nipples. Their pubic hair was shaved once a week by the midwife.

(Adoption Rights Now (2013) *Report into the history of adoption in Ireland since 1922, and Sean Ross Abbey, Castlepollard, and Bessborough Mother & Baby Homes*. pp.2–3. **https://cf.broadsheet.ie/wp-content/uploads/2014/06/Report-into-adoption-practises-in-Ireland-since-1922.pdf**: accessed 30 October 2024)

As with the Magdalene institutions, mass burials were also found to have occurred at mother and baby homes, in this case for infants. At the Bon Secours Mother and Baby Home in Tuam, County Galway, which operated from 1925 to 1961, and which had previously existed as a workhouse from 1841 onwards, many burials of foetuses and children up to 3 years of age were found in an underground structure believed to be a septic tank in the grounds. For the majority of these children, no death or burial records were kept. The 'Commission of Investigation into Mother and Baby Homes and Certain Related Matters' (2015–20) established, via carbon dating of the remains, that they had died between the 1920s and 1950s, and that they were certainly not Famine burials, as some defending the institution had suggested. In total, 802 children were found to have died in the home at Tuam, with a further 176 former inhabitants of the home found to have died as children in neighbouring institutions. Of the children, 870 were illegitimate, with 80 per cent aged under a year. The Commission's final report was published in 2021, and included a similar investigation into many other former homes in the Republic (**www.gov.ie/en/publication/d4b3d-final-report-of-the-commission-of-investigation-into-mother-and-baby-homes/**).

Mother and baby homes also existed in Northern Ireland. An investigation into practices in the North was carried out on behalf of the Stormont Government's Department of Health by Queen's University and Ulster University, and published in 2021 (**www.health-ni.gov.uk/mother-and-baby-homes-and-magdalene-laundries-research-report**), which identified some 10,500 woman and teenage girls who passed through their doors between 1922 and 1990, at which point the last such home closed. At the time of writing, a consultation is underway to establish the parameters for an inquiry into mother and baby homes in the North, with the Northern Irish government already acknowledging that financial redress will be made to survivors who step forward to make a claim. A list of some of these homes is available at **www.childrenshomes.org.uk/list/MB15.shtml**.

From 3 October 2022, the Birth Information and Tracing Act 2022 (**www.irishstatutebook.ie/eli/2022/act/14/enacted/en/html**) has established that those in the Republic affected by adoption, who were boarded out, or who were the victims of an illegal birth registration (p.49), can now gain access to their original birth certificates, and information about their early life that may be held, a provision that can be extended to their next-of kin in certain circumstances. A tracing service has also been established, as well as a Contact Preference Register. For further details, visit the Birth Information and Tracing service at **www.birthinfo.ie**.

Daniel Loftus' Project Infant site at **https://projectinfant.ie** is a recently established project that hopes to transcribe the names of all the children

Peter Higginbotham's Children's Homes site has information on many mother and baby homes located in Ireland.

who died at mother and baby homes in Ireland, with ten homes listed at the time of writing, and more to follow in the future.

Finally, there were also mother and baby homes in Britain, with various agencies operating such institutions, including the Salvation Army (**www.salvationarmy.org.uk/mother-and-baby-homes**). Peter Higginbotham's Children's Homes site at **www.childrenshomes.org.uk/MB/** hosts more information on these.

Foundlings

The Dublin Foundling Hospital was founded in 1702, initially as a workhouse, and received many newborn babies, abandoned by their mothers, from all over Ireland. Most were the children of Roman Catholic mothers, who were then raised with a Protestant education, with their mothers then denied any further contact.

In 1876 William Dudley Wodsworth, the Inspector of Invalid Foundlings, published *A Brief History of the Ancient Foundling Hospital of Dublin, from the Year 1702, with some account of similar institutions abroad*. In this he noted the purposes of the institution – 'to prevent the exposure, death and actual murder of illegitimate children', and 'to educate and rear children taken charge of by the Institution in the Reformed or Protestant Faith, and thereby to strengthen and promote the Protestant interest in Ireland' – but commented that in both of these regards the hospital largely failed.

> **CASE STUDY:** The following is a typical punishment from the Dublin Foundling Hospital's early years as noted by Wodsworth from the institution's minutes from August 1732:
>
> > Ordered, – That William Mills be confined in the House of Correction, and whipt three several days; that he be then brought into the Workhouse, put in the Dungeon, and tyed with a chain to a piece of logg…
>
> > (Wodsworth, William Dudley. (1876) *A Brief History of the Ancient Foundling Hospital of Dublin, from the Year 1702, with some account of similar institutions abroad.* Dublin: Alexander Thom. p.27. **https://archive.org/details/briefhistoryofan00wods**: accessed 30 October 2024)
>
> Two months later Mills was noted to still be in the hospital's House of Correction, because 'the cloggs and chains' had yet to be provided for him.

Under the Poor Law Act introduced during the reign of Queen Anne in 1702, it was originally intended that poor children over 5 years of age would be detained and kept in service until aged 16 (this later changed to 12), at which point they would be apprenticed out to 'honest' Protestants. Through the system, girls would remain so bound until the age of 21, while boys remained bound until 24. The stipulation that they had to be at least 5 years old was dropped following subsequent acts, at which point the foundling hospital became swamped with babies from across Ireland, who were to be put through such schemes.

The hospital was a cruel institution, with those transgressing its rules sent to the 'blackhole' or 'dungeon' as punishment, as well as receiving beatings with canes and birches. Children looked after by Catholic nurses had Protestantism forcibly imposed on them, with one witness noting that on Fridays 'they would not use the broth prepared with meat as it was, and it used to be poured down their throats against their will'.

Wodsworth's report includes copies of many sample letters received from mothers trying to reclaim their children, as well as entries from the apprentices register from 1824 to 1833, showing the fate of any of those so employed, with the following just some of the examples:

Jane Barker	Seduced, struck off.
Sarah Trew	Married, struck off.
John Wheatley	Returned from master – badly treated.
Robert Snow	Eloped and turned Papist.
Eliza Stephens	John Mathews reported that she had misconducted herself with William Stokes and left her master's service.
Mary Templeton	Eloped, and turned Prostitute.
Mary Page	Eloped, in consequence of her mistress having accused her of improper intercourse with her master, and went to live with Abraham Black, ever since which she has conducted herself with great propriety.
Fanny James	Worked too hard by master.
William Perry	'Under care of Police', having identified and prosecuted one of a party of 'Whitefeet' who attacked his master's house.

The hospital had a horrendous survival rate prior to 1829, its year of closure, with over 41,000 deaths, some 80 per cent of the children admitted into its custody. A second foundling hospital operated in Cork from 1747, located on Leitrim Street. Following its opening many children were for a time exchanged between the two hospitals to prevent their Catholic parents from gaining access to them, to prevent any obstruction in their being raised as Protestants. While the survival rate at this smaller institution was higher, some of its young girls were later sent from the institution to Australia to work as domestic servants, along with many selected from the nation's poorhouses, foreshadowing the later 'home children' scheme established by the British government (see p.51).

The Dublin Foundling Hospital later became the South Dublin Poorhouse from 1838, while the Cork hospital continued its work until 1854, when the site was purchased by Murphy's Brewery.

For more on the story of the Dublin institution read *The Least of These: The Tragic Story of Dublin's Foundling Hospital* by Mark B. Roe (The History Press Ireland, 2022).

Orphans

Abandoned or orphaned children were often sent to church-run orphanages to be raised. One of the oldest, Kirwan House (**www.kirwanhouse.com**), was operated from 1791 by the Protestant based Church of Ireland in Dublin as a Female Orphan House. Young girls who had been orphaned would be sent to the institution to be given an Anglican education, irrespective of what religion they had pursued prior to entry, and to be trained as domestic servants.

By the mid-twentieth century the institution, also referred to as Park House, was taking in both boys and girls, but in the late 1950s the remaining thirteen orphans were transferred to the local parsonage, and the building subsequently knocked down. With only three children still in the care of the institution in 1987, the decision was taken to wind down its role as an orphanage and for the home's funds to be converted into a trust fund.

CASE STUDY: The original admission register for the Female Orphan House at Kirwan House from 1791 to 1805 has been made available online at **www.historyeye.ie/_files/ugd/58e9cf_ad3cabe3dccc47758da297d953ea8e2e.pdf**. In the register there are comments as to what became of the orphans after they had entered, with the following some typical examples:

- Sarah Ogden was a 9-year-old Protestant English girl who entered the orphanage on 1 January 1791. She was noted to have been 'apprenticed as a servant to Miss Glesen, London, 3 June 1796. We have had good accounts of her.'
- 6-year-old Mary Reardon was a Roman Catholic from the parish of St Michael's, who entered the orphanage on 1 November 1802, with the comment recorded that she was 'dismissed for bad conduct' on 1 August 1814.
- 9-year-old Roman Catholic girl Elizabeth Doyle, from Delgany, Wicklow, entered the orphanage on 1 December 1803, but later 'eloped from the house' on 20 June 1809.
- 7-year-old Kilkenny Protestant girl Elizabeth King entered the institution on 1 March 1805, and was later 'apprenticed to her sister' in March 1918.

For more on the institution's history visit **www.historyeye.ie/female-orphan-house**.

Many orphanages were also set up across the country by the Roman Catholic Church, and by philanthropic individuals and charities. From 1858, reformatories were also established for youths aged 12–16 who were convicted of criminal conduct, and industrial schools from 1868 to train young orphans (as well as criminals under 12) with useful industrial and agricultural skills to help them secure work, before they were discharged at the age of 16. Most were run by the Catholic Church, but a small number of similar facilities run by the Church of Ireland were also established. Details of most institutions can be gleaned from Peter Higginbotham's Children's Homes platform (p.38), including details on where to source surviving records, although many will be subject to historical closure periods for access, usually for one hundred years.

Despite the existence of such orphanages, reformatories and industrial schools, the majority of orphans were in fact handled through the poor relief system, with orphaned children fostered out into local care. Information on such cases can be sought from surviving board of guardians minutes held at county archive offices in the Republic, or via PRONI in Northern Ireland. During the Famine the workhouse system was swamped with orphaned children, with some 90,000 estimated to be in care in 1851, and some were sent overseas. An article on children orphaned by the Famine and deported to Canada is available at **www.thecanadianencyclopedia.ca/en/article/irish-famine-orphans-in-canada**; the 'Immigrants at Grosse Île Quarantine Station, 1832–1937' database detailing many who were quarantined upon arrival in Quebec can be useful for research at **www.bac-lac.gc.ca/eng/discover/immigration/immigration-records/immigrants-grosse-ile-1832–1937/Pages/immigrants-grosse-ile.aspx**.

From 1769, children who had been orphaned as a result of fathers serving in the military being killed in action, or dying by other means while in service, could be sent to the Hibernian Society of the Orphans and Children of Soldiers in Phoenix Park, Dublin, later named the Royal Hibernian Military School. The school became the Irish equivalent of the Royal Military Asylum in Chelsea, established in 1801, which from 1892 became the Duke of York's Royal Military School. Pupils at the school would gain a military education, with many subsequently signing up to serve the Crown forces, particularly in the latter half of the nineteenth century, with over half enlisting.

Admission records from the institution can be searched in Findmypast's 'Ireland, Royal Hibernian Military School Staff and Pupils 1847–1932' collection. It should be noted that originally the school catered for both boys and girls, but in 1853 a separate establishment was established for girls at Chapelizod, called Drummond School.

CASE STUDY: Alexander William Halliday was born on the island of Bermuda on 16 August 1866. His father, also Alexander Halliday, was a soldier of the 2nd Battalion of the 2nd Regiment of Foot, and died in Bermuda on 31 January 1866, seven months before his son was born. His widowed mother, Teresa Mooney, was a Dubliner, and after remarrying, to another corporal in the same regimental battalion, she returned to Dublin (p.11).

On 1 August 1878, young Alexander, aged just 11 years and 11 months, was admitted by her mother and stepfather to the Royal Hibernian Military School. The enrolment record held at the National Archives, and available on Findmypast, confirms his date of birth, and states that his height was 4ft 4in, his weight as 4st 8lb, his chest as 24.5 inches, and his religion as Established Church (Church of Ireland). By the time he left he had gained one mark for good conduct, and no trade had been learned by him.

Aged just 13 years and 11 months, Alexander then officially joined the 48th Brigade on 17 August 1880, with his attestation witnessed by Staff Sergeant Michael Hogan. His medical just a few days earlier in Dublin on the 13th provides another description of him again at this age. He was apparently aged 14, was 4ft 9¼in tall, had a chest measurement of 27 inches, a fresh complexion, blue grey eyes, brown hair and was Church of England by way of religion. He had a scar on the back of his neck and one on the back of his right hand.

Aged 14, Alexander signed up as a private in the 1st Battalion of the 2nd Regiment of Foot, his father's former regiment, with whom he saw service until 1902, including a period in India. Following his discharge from the army he initially became a motorman, and then a tram driver in Dublin.

In 1913, Alexander was one of the tram drivers who abandoned their trams, kicking off the Dublin Lockout (p.138).

Finally, Findmypast hosts the 'Deserted Children Dublin' collection, which may be of interest; it listing some 500 children taken into the care by the Dublin Metropolitan Police Force between 1850 and 1854.

Adoption

Prior to Partition, and in its immediate aftermath, there was no state-sponsored form of adoption in Ireland, with the majority of children requiring care being put out to fosterage. Foster parents would raise the children in agreement with the agency authorising it, or by private agreement, but had no parental rights. However, it was possible to adopt privately, as facilitated through third parties such as doctors, nurses, lawyers, or ministers of religion.

State sponsored adoption was first formally legalised in Northern Ireland with the creation of the Adoption of Children Act (NI) in 1929, which followed a similar act passed in England three years earlier. Through the 1929 act, prospective parents in most cases had to be at least 21 years older than the child to be adopted, and had to be resident in Northern Ireland. A new adoption register was created, and following an adoption the word 'adopted' was to be entered beside the original birth registration entry in the birth register. A child could be adopted right up to the age of 21. Despite this new state-based system for adoption, it remained possible to adopt privately in the North until 1989.

Following the Adoption (Northern Ireland) Order 1987 coming into force in October 1989, it has been possible for anyone adopted in Northern Ireland, and who is aged over 18, to apply to the Registrar General in Belfast for a copy of their original birth certificate, and to learn about the circumstances of their adoption. The General Register Office for Northern Ireland has a detailed adoption guide for adoptees wishing to trace birth parents, including information on how to sign up to join the Adoption Contact Register. Entitled 'Tracing and contacting birth relatives and adopted adults', it can be accessed at **www.nidirect.gov.uk/articles/tracing-and-contacting-birth-relatives-and-adopted-adults**. The site discusses the various methods for obtaining an original birth certificate, with different rules for those born before or after 1987 – online application forms are also available. To order an adoption certificate, visit **https://geni.nidirect.gov.uk** or **www.nidirect.gov.uk/articles/ordering-life-event-certificates**. Further guidance can also be found via Adoption Search Reunion at **www.adoptionsearchreunion.org.uk/search/righttosearch/righttosearchni.htm**.

In the Free State adoption was also a private act, with illegitimate children often offered up for adoption after their mothers had given birth in mother and baby homes. By the middle of the century cases of illegal adoptions were being facilitated by adoption agencies forging birth certificates to show the names of the adoptive parents as the child's birth parents (such an act had been against the law in Ireland since 1874), while some adoptions were facilitated to couples based in the United States, providing a lucrative source of income for the agencies involved.

Shortly after becoming a republic, Ireland's Adoption Act of 1952 established a new state based adoption agency called An Bord Uchtála, which facilitated the adoption of orphans or illegitimate children aged

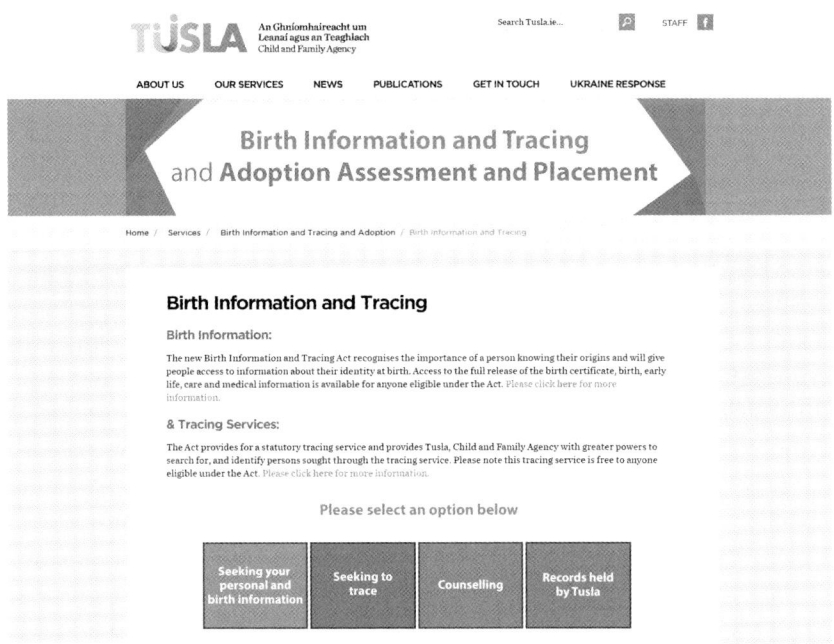

The Irish Government's TUSLA agency can assist with birth information and tracing services.

between 6 months and 7 years; this age limit was extended upwards to 9 years of age in 1964, and removed from 1974. The 1952 act stipulated that 'the applicant or applicants shall be of the same religion as the child and his parents or, if the child is illegitimate, his mother', and resident within the state; this was extended in 1974 to permit adoptions by couples of mixed religion.

GRO Ireland offers online application forms at **www.welfare.ie/en/Pages/General-Register-Office.aspx** for those wishing to obtain a certified copy of an entry in its Adopted Children Register. For a guide on how to trace birth parents you will need to consult the Health Service Executive site at **www.hse.ie/eng**. Type in 'Tracing Services' in the search box at the top right of the screen for the relevant guide, which also includes details of various support services you may require. The Republic's Child and Family Agency, Tusla (**www.tusla.ie**), holds records from many adoption societies. A list is provided at **www.tusla.ie/services/birth-information-and-tracing-and-adoption/information-and-tracing/records-held-by-tusla/**.

For Irish children adopted in Britain, advice can be sought from Adoption Search Reunion at **www.adoptionsearchreunion.org.uk**, or in Scotland, through Birthlink at **www.birthlink.org.uk**.

Child Migrants

Not all orphaned children were adopted or fostered, with some being transported overseas. During the Famine, some 4,000 Irish orphans were sent to Australia through what later became known as the Earl Grey Pauper Immigration Scheme, named after Earl Grey, the British Secretary of State for the colonies. The scheme's purpose was to clear the workhouses of children during the crisis, with the orphans selected, mostly girls aged 14–19, sent to Australia from October 1848 to August 1850 to work as domestic labour. Not all survived the journey, and some were abused on reaching their new homes. The scheme ultimately ended due to opposition from the colonies, which objected to Britain transporting its problems to the other side of the world.

In 1869 a further scheme was devised for the British Home Office by London based Annie MacPherson to send orphaned and destitute children overseas to Australia, Canada, New Zealand and South Africa. Not only was it believed that their new environment could be good for them, it also helped to alleviate a shortage of labour. Those sent overseas were known as 'home children', but their placements, which continued for a century up to 1970 from Britain, became increasingly controversial. It was later revealed that some of those who had been relocated had been exploited in their new homes, and in some cases physically or sexually abused. Worse still, many children and parents had been lied to about their respective fates, with some parents believing that their children had died, and vice versa, when that was not the case, prompting a formal apology from the British government in 2010.

While the majority of home children were sent from Britain, children were also sent from Ireland, in the years prior to Partition. A search on the Findmypast hosted collection 'Canada, Home Children Immigration Records Index, 1869–1930' shows 138 returns for child migrants from the city of Dublin alone, including many sent from the north and south

> **CASE STUDY:** A typical example from Library and Archives Canada's Home Children Records database cites the arrival in Quebec in 1870 of nine children from Londonderry, who sailed on the *Peruvian*. The eldest were 18-year-old Susan Casey and Eliza S. Sherdin, the youngest was 11-year-old Ann Regan.
>
> Another entry from the Fegan Distributing Home in Toronto noted the arrival in 1890 of 18-year-old T.G. Sullivan on board the *Sarnia*, but with a note appended stating that Sullivan had 'gone home to Ireland in 1894'.

Dublin poor law unions. The database also includes details of hundreds sent from poor law unions and charitable institutions across Ireland.

The Library and Archives Canada website has additional resources and databases for home children which can be accessed via the 'A to Z tools and guides' page at **https://library-archives.canada.ca/eng/ collection/research-help/all-tools-guides/Pages/all-tools-guides.aspx**.

For those who may have travelled to Australia, rather than Canada, a useful starting point is a State Library of Victoria guide on the topic available at **https://guides.slv.vic.gov.au/adoption/childmigrants**.

While the scheme ceased in the Free State following Partition, children continued to be sent from Northern Ireland. The Northern Ireland Historical Institutional Abuse Inquiry, which sat from 2014–2015, concluded that 130 such children had been subsequently sent to Australia from the North between 1922 and 1995, with most sent immediately after the Second World War. Following the inquiry an official apology was made to victims in the Stormont Parliament on 11 March 2022 by the main political parties and several of the institutions which had participated in the scheme.

For more on the plight of home children, visit the UK based Child Migrants Trust platform at **www.childmigrantstrust.org**.

Marital Issues

For many couples in Ireland, marriage was a resounding success, but not all spouses ended up living 'happily ever after'. In certain cases marriages could be annulled before they had even got off the ground, while some of those that did proceed could turn out to be loveless affairs, producing many potential consequences.

In Ireland a marriage prior to 1845 was recognised as valid so long as a promise to marry had been conveyed before a clergyman who had been ordained by a bishop, essentially Anglican and Catholic priests. The calling of banns in advance of a wedding, much despised by both Protestant and Catholic communities, could also be dispensed with by securing a licence from the Anglican minister instead. The Church of Ireland's marriages were technically the only ones that were legally valid, being performed by the state church, but in practice toleration did extend to other denominations. There were some prohibitions, however, with Catholic priests forbidden to perform weddings between Protestants from 1697 to 1871, or mixed marriages between a Catholic and a Protestant prior to 1793. Presbyterian ministers by their very nature were not ordained by bishops, and thus were initially barred from performing such ceremonies, but a 'fudge' was introduced through legislation in

1738, whereby Presbyterians were able to oversee the creation of 'marriage contracts'. From 1782 marriages between two Presbyterians by Presbyterian ministers were legally sanctioned by the state.

> **TIP:** If you cannot find a marriage for a dissenting Protestant or a Roman Catholic ancestor, try the marriage registers of the local Church of Ireland parish, which as the state church may have registered or documented such a union.

Unlike the Protestant churches, the Roman Catholic Church continued to recognise marriage as a sacrament. Following the Tametsi decree of 1563, a requirement was made that a marriage had to be performed before a priest and two witnesses, preferably with parental consent. Mixed marriages with Protestants were permitted if the union was carried out by a Catholic priest. The Tametsi provisions were not fully implemented in parts of Ireland until the late eighteenth and nineteenth centuries, at which point the calling of banns became a more stringent requirement in Catholic ceremonies.

One of the consequences of the Marriage (Ireland) Act of 1844 was the creation of civil marriage by the state for the first time, and many couples wishing to marry across different denominations could now do so without any religious interference, although this could potentially cause issues subsequently with the baptism of any children. Within the Catholic Church, a controversial change to its own laws on mixed marriage was introduced in 1908 after the passing of the Ne Temere decree, which required mixed marriages to be performed by a Catholic priest; many such priests would only agree to perform such unions if the couple agree to raise any children born to them as Roman Catholic.

In addition to marriages performed by ordained priests and tolerated Presbyterians, prior to 1845 many marriages were carried out irregularly across Ireland by ministers known as 'couple beggars', 'tack 'ems', or 'buckle the beggars', without prior publication by banns or the issue of a marriage licence, making their services considerably cheaper. These came from all religious denominations, with ministers who had fallen out of favour with their respective churches, and in some cases, who had never been ordained in the first place. From 1725 onwards they could be prosecuted and put to death, although within thirty years the maximum sentence imposed was reduced to seven years transportation, or simply imprisonment.

Some couple beggars did hold official positions within their respective churches, but made money privately by carrying out irregular marriages.

While most records of such ministers were unfortunately destroyed at the PRO in 1922, two volumes of marriage registers have survived which were kept by a Lutheran priest in Dublin, Johann George Frederick Schulze, which document some 6,000 irregular marriages carried out by him from 1806 to 1837. The registers are kept at the General Register Office in Roscommon, but a transcription was published in 2015 in 'Irregular Marriages in Dublin before 1837' by Harry McDowell. The original volumes were also microfilmed in 1953 by the Church of Jesus Christ of Latter-day Saints, and can be called up at the FamilySearch Library on microfilm 101771. The 1844 Marriages (Ireland) Act put an end to the work of couple beggars.

> **CASE STUDY:** A short notice from the *Newry Telegraph* of Friday, 31 July 1829 (p.2) showed the interest that the public had in the stories of couple beggars:
>
> > Mr Joseph Wood, the celebrated 'Couple-beggar', died on Sunday evening of fever, at his house in Haymarket, Dublin. His business was so extensive, that it is said he married, within the last sixteen years, no less than five thousand couples, being on an average upwards of three hundred for each year!
>
> Following Wood's death his widow Jane continued to run the marriage business he had established in Dublin. The business finally came to an end with the passing of the Marriages (Ireland) Act 1844.

While many couples were happily married, regularly or irregularly, there were situations where a promise to marry having been made was subsequently not kept. This was in breach of the rules set down by various church denominations, and could be prosecuted by their ecclesiastical courts, although in many cases the most severe punishment imposed could be for a supposed offender to be removed from the congregation.

From the state's perspective the Church of Ireland's consistory courts in each diocese were the ruling authority when it came to the legality of marriage, and it heard cases on a wide range of subjects from adultery to separations. Sadly, very little has survived of these records, with available material held at the National Archives of Ireland for the dioceses of Dublin (NAI: 4/271/37), Tuam from 1740 to 1742 (NAI: M6833) and Killaloe from 1707 to 1868 (NAI: 4/201/13), with additional material for Killaloe held at the British Library in London covering the period from 1671 to 1824 (BL: Add MSS 31881–2).

From the eighteenth century onwards breach of promise cases began to be heard in the civil courts. Such actions were based on the premise of it being a breach of contract law, with an arrangement previously agreed to then subsequently dishonoured, for which the aggrieved party would

> **CASE STUDY:** An unusual breach of promise of marriage case at the Cork Assizes on Tuesday, 24 March 1835 was reported in the *Southern Reporter and Cork Commerical Courier* two days later.
>
> The plaintiff, a 40-year-old unmarried woman called Eliza Roche had proof, in the form of a letter dated to February 1834, that she had been asked to marry 60-year-former hotel keeper in Cork called Conway, who was a widower. The pair had had a relationship for four years. Eliza replied positively to the proposal, but as her father had recently passed away in May 1833, she asked that any marriage should not occur until her father had been buried twelve months. The couple began to make preparations for the marriage, including purchasing the wedding attire and drawing up a guest list, and the date of 29 April was agreed upon as the wedding day. Conway even sent a gold watch to Eliza as a gift, in advance of the wedding.
>
> On the Sunday before the wedding, Conway fell sick, 'under increased determination of blood to the head', and it was stated by his doctor that if he attempted to marry he would not last six months, with Conway agreeing that if he did so, 'it would be flying in the face of Providence'. Upon being informed of his change of mind, Eliza suggested that they still marry, but after the ceremony she would live with him as a sister in his house to look after him, but he again refused. She subsequently returned the gold watch. Within days, Conway was then seen back at his work at the Bazaar, with the appearance of being in full health again. The case for damages against him was then pursued.
>
> The judge, in summarising the case before the jury, stated that there was clearly a breach of marriage freely admitted to by Conway, and that the fact of his illness did not preclude him from paying damages. At the same time, he clearly viewed the arrangement between the couple to be unusual, and noted wryly: 'But what is the loss to this lady? Marrying an old man subject to apoplexy!'
>
> Nevertheless, he did believe that she had suffered wounded pride as a consequence of the breach of promise, and should be entitled to moderate damages. The jury, instructed to determine the level of such damages, settled on £300 damages to the plaintiff, and six pence in costs.

be entitled to sue for damages. Many such cases were brought to the courts by women concerned about their ability to marry in the future, fearing reputational damage, with newspapers regularly providing coverage.

Cases of adultery were also heard in the church courts, with the Presbyterian community in particular keen to investigate such cases, as through Presbyterian theology it could be the precursor to a divorce, which the church permitted. Such cases can be examined in the church's kirk session registers, held at PRONI or at the Presbyterian Historical Society of Ireland in Belfast. In the civil courts, details of adulterous affairs could be heard as part of criminal conversation cases (p.60), as a forerunner to divorce proceedings.

A superb publication covering marital law in Ireland, including cases of breaches of promise and adultery, is *Marriage in Ireland 1660–1925* by Maria Luddy and Mary O'Dowd (Cambridge University Press, 2020).

Separation and Divorce

Under Brehon Law (p.75) it was possible for a divorce to be granted by mutual consent between spouses in the higher echelons of Irish society, and for either or both to remarry. A woman could divorce her husband and retain occupancy of her marital home, and there were many potential grounds for divorce, ranging from a husband's homosexuality or potential infertility, to the husband slandering her or assaulting her and leaving a mark. Reasons for a husband seeking to divorce a wife included adultery, an abortion undertaken without agreement, or if theft had been committed. As part of a divorce, a financial settlement could be agreed upon based on what each party had brought into their union at the time of marriage.

The canon law of the early Christian church initially worked in parallel to the Brehon Law system, and in its earliest period did facilitate divorce by mutual consent, but over time the Church moved its stance towards a position where marriage itself was a sacrament, as confirmed at the Council of Trent from 1545 to 1563. Following the Reformation, the Protestant churches broke away from this idea, instead proclaiming marriage to be a form of contract.

In the modern period, all of the Irish churches permitted an annulment of a marriage if it could be proved that such a union had created a bigamous situation, if there was coercion of a spouse to marry, if the spouses were too closely related (breaching the rules of consanguinity as laid out in the Old Testament book of Leviticus), or if there was an inability to consummate a union due to some form of incapacity (for example, if one of the spouses was insane). Beyond this the churches differed over by what alternative means, if any, a marriage could be ended.

The Roman Catholic Church, the largest denomination on the island, continued to insist that a marriage was for life, and could not be dissolved other than by the death of one of the spouses. The Presbyterian faith took a more liberal approach following its subscription to the Westminster Confession of Faith in 1646, permitting a spouse a divorce if betrayed by an act of adultery or desertion, with such cases documented in kirk session and presbytery papers. However, the Church of Ireland, which controlled the state's ecclesiastical courts, permitted a divorce only if one of the partners had been missing for seven years, and was thus believed to be dead. No matter the positions of the other churches, if a couple separated by means other than through the state court, and subsequently remarried, they could be open to a charge of bigamy, even if they had fulfilled their own church's requirements.

While a full divorce proved difficult to secure for many, there was a form of legally sanctioned separation that was entertained by the state. Separation or limited divorce by 'a mensa et thoro' (literally meaning 'from table and bed', i.e. 'from bed and board') permitted the couple to lead independent lives if an act of adultery was proven, but it did not

The Catholic Church did not permit divorce in Ireland, while the Protestant churches did so in certain circumstances. Irrespective of religion, however, couples could separate by 'a mensa et thoro'.

CASE STUDY: One of the more scandalous divorce cases in Ireland concerned Lord Valentine Brown Lawless, 2nd Baron Cloncurry in Kildare, and his wife Eliza Georgiana Morgan, Baroness Cloncurry, his first wife. The couple had married in 1803, and by 1805 had produced two children. In 1806, however, the baroness committed adultery with a friend of her husband, Sir John Bennett Piers, 6th Baronet of Tristernagh Abbey in Westmeath, at their Kildare home of Lyons House. When Cloncurry discovered the affair, he sued Piers at the Court of King's Bench in Dublin on 19 February 1807 through a case of criminal conversation (p.60).

The press spared little detail about the extraordinary circumstances of the adultery. The *Belfast News-Letter* of 23 and 25 February 1807 noted how Sir John had been entertained for dinner at the baron's property on a several occasions, and had written to the 19-year-old baroness subsequently professing his love for her. On another occasion he then carried out the following act of 'daring effrontery', as the paper called it:

> He first took the precaution of opening a door which led into an apartment adjoining the drawing-room, in which Lady Cloncurry sat, and being satisfied that no person was there, he shut the door, and took particular pains to put down the covering over the keyhole. However, it so happened, with all Sir John's precaution, he overlooked an Italian artist, who was then employed in one angle of the room, painting the ceiling, what followed after shutting the door will best be proved from the event; he began by telling her from the hopeless passion he entertained, he would be obliged to fly his country and live in perpetual exile, but this being unavailable, there is little doubt but by brutal force (for he is a man of uncommon strength), he accomplished his design. Certain it is the painter having had occasion to come into the room, found her under the most suspicious circumstances, with her dress very much discomposed. Sir John then left the house, and Lady Cloncurry retired to her chamber.

The paper went on to note that Piers subsequently took up residence close to her, and that an adulterous relationship developed, it further noting that he was:

> assiduous in his attentions to Lady Cloncurry, he met her at all places of public resort, he visited her at her lodgings, and there is no doubt but before the end of the month he accomplished all his designs. Such scenes would be proved to have occurred here as would put the matter completely out of doubt; she wore his picture, and a locket with his hair in it was found after in her bed.
>
> In the following month Cloncurry himself witnessed his wife with Sir John Piers out walking, having excused herself from a meal pretending to be ill. When confronted, the baroness confessed to her adultery. Cloncurry soon caught up with his friend Sir John, who was out shooting game, and on the pretence that he would take part also he took the gun from him, at which point he pointed it at his friend and said: 'Piers, I do not wish to destroy you, nether do I wish to destroy my wife's reputation; before you ruin her peace of mind, or my honour, fly this place; God forgive you; God bless you.'
>
> Piers fled from the scene, but following an allegation that he had subsequently written a letter to challenge Cloncurry to a duel, a warrant was issued for his arrest, prompting him to flee to Douglas, Isle of Man. At this point, Cloncurry initiated his criminal conviction action, which resulted in a record sum in damages of £20,000 to be paid to him.
>
> Cloncurry then proceeded to initiate a divorce action against his wife. A decree of a mensa et thoro was granted by the ecclesiastical court, which Lady Cloncurry unsuccessfully challenged in the civil courts in November 1810. This paved the way for Cloncurry to have his divorce bill heard in the House of Lords from February 1811, which was granted royal assent on 3 July.
>
> A week later, Cloncurry remarried to the widowed Emily Douglas, the mother of the 4th Earl of Milltown.

break the bond of marriage itself. For many this was as far as the legal proceedings went, but for those seeking a full divorce via Parliament, they had to first obtain such a separation. Prior to the disestablishment of the Church of Ireland as the state church, the procedure was facilitated by the Anglican courts, before being transferred to the civil courts from 1870. Unfortunately, because of the destruction of the Public Record Office and the Four Courts in 1922, very few court records have survived for such cases.

The state, however, did provide for another alternative, in the form of a divorce granted by a private act of the Irish Parliament, with the first case permitted on such a basis in 1730. To gain such a divorce, one of the spouses would first have to initiate a 'criminal conversation' case in the Court of King's Bench in Dublin, the word 'conversation' here being an obsolete euphemism for sexual intercourse. This was effectively an action to sue the person with whom his or her spouse had committed adultery, to seek damages for what had essentially been an act of 'trespass' on their 'property'. Cases of criminal conversation continued to be heard in Northern Ireland until the Matrimonial Causes Act (Northern Ireland) 1939 ended the practice, and in the Republic until it was abolished by the Family Law Act 1981.

Having secured damages, the same plaintiff would proceed to seek a judicial separation a mensa et thoro. Once this was granted, a divorce bill could then be applied for through Parliament, initially through the Irish Parliament, and then from 1801 onwards, through the British Parliament at Westminster.

Following Partition, in the new Free State divorce was still technically possible, but effectively forbidden, with the Catholic Church's influence holding sway; from 1937 it was specifically banned by Article 41 of the Irish Constitution. It was not until 1996, in the aftermath of a narrow referendum victory in the Republic on 24 November 1995, that divorce was finally permitted as a means to end a marriage in civil law, following an amendment to the Constitution. From this point onwards a divorce could be secured if a couple had lived separately for four out of the five previous years, changing in 2019 to two out of the previous three.

In Northern Ireland, divorce continued to be facilitated through parliamentary bills, following a court based separation agreement, with the Northern Parliament hearing its first case in 1925, the divorce of Isabella Wright, née Weir, and her husband John Wright, two Roman Catholics from County Sligo who had resettled in Portadown, County Armagh. Between 1925 and 1939, sixty-three divorce cases were heard in the Northern Parliament, with over half from Belfast alone. In 1939 the parliamentary procedure for divorce ended, along with the need for cases of criminal conversation, with cases now heard by the Northern Ireland High Court for the first time. From this point the rate of divorce increased, but with the cost of a divorce considerably higher than in Britain, the rate of divorce remained much lower. Today, a divorce can be granted in Northern Ireland following two years' separation with the consent of the other spouse, or five years without, on the grounds of unreasonable behaviour, adultery, or desertion.

In addition to press coverage of Irish divorce proceedings, coverage of divorce bills taken through the Westminster Parliament prior to Partition can be read through the ProQuest UK Parliamentary Papers platform (p.81). Various surviving case papers from Northern parliamentary divorces are available from PRONI, including divorce files from 1926 to 1988 under MAT/3, and divorce files for poor persons from 1945 to 1954 under MAT/4. In addition are many private papers and Northern Ireland government papers covering aspects of the divorce process.

While the facilitation of divorce is a fairly recent event in the Republic, the National Archives of Ireland has some papers on questions surrounding the issue over the last century. The online catalogue also throws up some interesting examples from cases considered by the Department of Foreign Affairs, such as 'Divorce proceedings by Madam Macbeth in France question of nationality of her husband' (January 1933; DFA/2/1/100) and 'Mr J. Haan of Essen, Germany. Divorce proceedings against wife – question of renouncing his Saorstát citizenship' (March 1934; DFA/2/31/60).

The subject of divorce in Ireland, before and after Partition, and in both the North and South, is covered extensively in Diane Urquhart's publication *Irish Divorce: A History* (Cambridge University Press, 2020).

Bigamy

While it was possible to separate a mensa et thoro, this did prevent any subsequent remarriage from occurring if a full divorce was not secured, for the separated spouses were still connected through their matrimonial bond. This did not stop some folk from acting as if they had divorced, with many going on to marry again, with such ceremonies often carried out by 'couple beggars' (p.53). In so doing, the remarrying spouse was committing the crime of bigamy. From 1635 this was classified as a

> **CASE STUDY:** On Friday, 22 April 1774, the Dublin published *Saunders's News-Letter* noted that at the Cork assizes a week earlier, on 15 April, a John Cavendish Maudesly was convicted of bigamy and sentenced to seven years' transportation.
>
> Sentence was not carried out until almost a year later, however, with the *Hibernian Chronicle* of Wednesday, 29 March 1775 noting that on the previous day in Cork, 'twelve Convicts from the City and County Gaols, among whom was John Cavendish Maudesly, for Bigamy, were put on Board a Vessel at our Quay, in order to be transported to North America.'

capital crime in Ireland, although from 1725 an alternative punishment was established in the form of transportation to the British colonies, with such a sentence from 1829 set at seven years.

Although the official punishment of transportation ended in 1868 (p.93), in practice, sentencing varied across the country before that, with some imprisoned as an alternative, with or without hard labour, and with sentences of varying lengths. Bigamists were usually found to have come from Ireland's working classes, and were usually men.

Divorce or separation was for many people simply not an option. Quite apart from the expense and the time it would take, there was also the question of economics for many households. It was often the situation in a household that everyone had to work to keep things afloat, and for women with children in particular it would be difficult to walk away, or for a husband to walk away, from a marriage. Such circumstances could unfortunately lead to instances of domestic violence.

> **CASE STUDY:** On 9 February 1891, a tweed manufacturer called Roland Haigh, based at Killaloe, County Clare, married a Mary Walker at the Church of Ireland parish church in Bray, County Wicklow. The civil record shows nothing out of the ordinary with the marriage, it noting that Haigh was a bachelor and Walker a spinster, with both of full age (i.e. aged 21 or over).
>
> The *Carlow Nationalist* of Saturday, 12 December 1891, however, noted a hearing at the Leinster winter assizes in Carlow, telling a completely different story about the marriage, where it was established that Haigh had previously married in Huddersfield, Yorkshire, in September 1880. In Haigh's defence, a Baptist minister, Rev. E.J. Scannell, informed the judge that he had been present at that wedding ceremony, but that in Huddersfield there was a superstition that married people who were seven years separated could marry again. He further added that Haigh was a man of good character.
>
> The astonished judge was not impressed, noting that England 'must be a very barbarous country. I assure you that there is no such superstition here.' He then told Haigh that he had been 'brought up in a country so involved in darkness and bewilderment as to the laws of marriage', and that 'whatever superstition there might be about Bradford or Huddersfield it was certain that it did not exist in that backward place called Killaloe'.
>
> Haigh was sentenced to eighteen months' imprisonment with hard labour.

For more on the topic read *Marriage in Ireland 1660–1925* by Maria Luddy and Mary O'Dowd (Cambridge University Press, 2020).

Homosexuality

One area where marriage was not even a possibility until recently was within Ireland's historical gay communities. Civil partnerships, essentially non-church sanctioned unions, were introduced in the Republic in January 2011, and although similar to marriage, they did not cater for issues surrounding the guardianship, adoption or custody of children. Same sex marriage was introduced in the country just under five years later, in November 2015, following a referendum earlier in the year in May, which led to the Marriage Act 2015. A consequence of this new act has been that no further civil partnerships have been permitted in the South since its implementation, although those in such partnerships retain all rights that they have gained, with their unions still recognised.

In Northern Ireland, civil partnerships were introduced in December 2005, at the same time as the rest of the UK, but it would be just over fourteen years later that same sex marriage was finally introduced, in January 2020. Rather than being introduced on the back of a referendum to show popular support, it was instead implemented by the British Secretary of State for Northern Ireland, Julian Smith, following the ongoing failure of the Northern Irish parties to agree on its introduction. Unlike the Republic, in Northern Ireland it remains possible to choose between a civil partnership or a same-sex marriage.

The battle to achieve such rights was a long drawn-out affair, with the attitude of the state towards homosexuality in Ireland one of hostility and intolerance, prior to its eventual decriminalisation in both parts of the island. As a consequence of such opposition, it was impossible for our gay ancestors and relatives to enjoy the same rights as are currently enjoyed by relatives today. Indeed, it was not unknown for those who were gay to marry and to have families; Dublin born playwright Oscar Wilde, imprisoned from 1895 to 1897 after conviction on charges of sodomy and gross indecency in England, had previously married Constance Lloyd in London in 1884, with whom he had two sons.

In 1634 the Irish Parliament had adopted into law the 1533 'Acte for the punishment of the vice of Buggerie', drawn up during the reign of Henry VIII over a century earlier in England. This noted the severe penalty that could be meted out to those found to be guilty:

> the offenders being hereof convict by verdict confession or outlawry, shall suffer such pains of death, and losses and penalties of their

good chattels debts lands tenements and hereditaments, as felons be accustomed to do, according to the Order of the Common Laws of this Realm.

(Raithby. John, ed. (1811). *The Statutes at Large, of England and of Great Britain: from Magna Carta to the Union of the Kingdoms of Great Britain and Ireland, Vol. 3*. London, G. Eyre and A. Strahan. p.145. **https://babel.hathitrust.org/cgi/pt?id=njp.32101075729275&seq=187**: accessed 30 October 2024)

Ironically and tragically, the Anglican bishop who had pushed for Ireland to adopt the act, Bishop John Atherton, was in fact the first person to be hanged in the country in 1640 under its provisions, after being found guilty of the act of sodomy with his steward and tithe proctor, John Childe, who was similarly executed.

The law was replaced by the British government in 1829 with the Offences Against the Person Act, although the death penalty was retained in statute for those convicted of the offence. It would not be until 1861, through a revised Offences Against the Person Act, that the death sentence was replaced with lengthy imprisonment. The updated legislation now stipulated three specific clauses for which prosecution could be pursued, in language that would be deemed unacceptable today:

Sodomy and bestiality
61. Whosoever shall be convicted of the abominable crime of buggery, committed either with mankind or with any animal, shall be liable … to be kept in penal servitude for life.

Attempt to commit an infamous crime
62. Whosoever shall attempt to commit the said abominable crime, or shall be guilty of any assault with intent to commit the same, or of any indecent assault upon any male person, shall be guilty of a misdemeanour, and being convicted thereof shall be liable … to be kept in penal servitude for any term not exceeding ten years.

Carnal knowledge defined
63. Whenever, upon the trial for any offence punishable under this Act, it may be necessary to prove carnal knowledge, it shall not be necessary to prove the actual emission of seed in order to constitute

a carnal knowledge, but the carnal knowledge shall be deemed complete upon proof of penetration only.

(Electronic Irish Statute Book (2024) Offences Against The Person Act, 1861.
www.irishstatutebook.ie/eli/1861/act/100/enacted/en/print: accessed 30 October 2024)

A further provision through the subsequent Criminal Law Amendment Act of 1885 also targeted those aiding in homosexual prostitution:

Outrages on decency
11. Any male person who, in public or private, commits, or is a party to the commission of, or procures or attempts to procure the commission by any male person of, any act of gross indecency with another male person, shall be guilty of a misdemeanour, and being convicted thereof shall be liable at the discretion of the court to be imprisoned for any term not exceeding two years, with or without hard labour.

(Electronic Irish Statute Book (2024) Criminal Law Amendment Act, 1885.
www.irishstatutebook.ie/eli/1885/act/69/enacted/en/print: accessed 30 October 2024)

The Cornwall case (see p.66) provides an example of the reputational damage that could be endured if a gay man, or one accused of being gay, was outed by others, but for the researcher it is often the accusation and the criminal consequences that are the only evidence that can be found in records of the lifestyle of those so accused – particularly if no letters or diaries exist to provide their own voices. However, even these documents can be controversial, as the case of Sir Roger Casement shows, the Protestant nationalist from County Antrim who was executed for treason in the aftermath of the Easter Rising. Following his arrest, three diaries dated to 1903, 1910 and 1911, purportedly written by Casement, and detailing various sexual encounters with other men, were used by the British government to smear his reputation to try to prevent any requests for clemency prior to his sentence being carried out. Today known as the 'Black Diaries', academics are still divided as to whether the journals were genuinely written by him, or if they were forgeries drawn up to discredit him.

CASE STUDY: A prominent scandal in Dublin in 1884 was that involving Gustavus Cornwall, who had been in post as Secretary of the city's General Post Office since April 1850. Cornwall was accused by William O'Brien MP in his publication *United Ireland* of having had a relationship with James Ellis French, the head of Dublin Castle's Criminal Investigation Department. Cornwall was suspended by the Post Office, and duly sued O'Brien, but lost the case.

Cornwall was then arrested on 12 July at his brother-in-law's house in Linlithgow, Scotland, and taken back to Dublin, charged with being guilty of 'felonious and unnatural crimes'. However, at the end of October he was tried and acquitted of all charges.

In the following year Cornwall then moved to have the earlier libel case overturned, but was only partially successful in clearing his name. His reputation still stained, the Post Office accepted his resignation, but refused to pay him a pension.

Some documents from the Cornwall case are held by the Postal Museum in London, England, with several illustrated online at **www.postalmuseum.org/blog/gustavus-cornwall/**.

The General Post Office on Dublin's O'Connell Street.

For women, lesbianism was not penalised in the same way by law as male homosexuality, but it was nevertheless deemed to be just as scandalous when outed, and can be equally difficult to determine from archival sources. In 1921, plans to extend the same punishments to women for same-sex sexual acts were considered for the Criminal Law Bill, but never implemented. Among those believed to have been lesbians in Ireland during the revolutionary period were Elizabeth O'Farrell from Dublin, who was sent by Patrick Pearse to seek terms of surrender from the British during the Easter Rising, and who lived together with fellow Cumann na mBan (p.147) member Julie Grenan for over thirty years, the two being subsequently buried beside each other at Glasnevin Cemetery.

Following Partition, both Irish territories maintained the prohibitions against gay men, with the strong influence of the Catholic Church in the South and the Protestant churches in the North informing the debate against those seeking tolerance. Throughout the 1970s and 1980s an emergent gay rights movement in Ireland, North and South, fought to have homosexuality decriminalised. It would not be until two landmark cases heard through the European Court of Human Rights that their objectives were finally secured in both the North and the South – in Northern Ireland through Dudgeon vs United Kingdom in 1981, which led to decriminalisation in 1982 through the Homosexual Offences (Northern Ireland) Order 1982, No. 1536 (N.I. 19), and in the Republic through a case brought against the state by Senator David Norris in 1988, leading to decriminalisation in 1993, via the Criminal Law (Sexual Offences) 1993 Act.

For the recent history of LGBT activism in Ireland over the last half century, the Irish Queer Archive (Cartlann Aerach na hÉireann) 1974–2005 at the National Library of Ireland may be able to assist, with the catalogue accessible via **https://catalogue.nli.ie/Collection/vtls000276865**.

Death

While the death of an individual was certainly the end of their life story, it may well have had consequences that impacted far and wide after their demise. The demise of a main breadwinner within the family could often provide a major economic blow to the remaining household, forcing many to claim for poor relief or admission to the workhouse (p.103), or to relocate to pastures new.

Death may well have followed a long illness, details of which may be noted on a post-1864 death certificate, with such a period of suffering allowing family members to prepare for the inevitable, but sometimes it occurred instantly or with little warning. Not all causes of death were immediately apparent, and in cases of unusual and suspicious deaths, the coroner may have been brought in to investigate.

The role of the coroner has existed in Ireland since medieval times, but was substantially reformed by the Coroners (Ireland) Act 1846, which established elected coroners for districts in each county of Ireland. The role was further professionalised into a full-time occupation by the Coroners (Ireland) Act 1881. Following the Local Government (Ireland) Act 1898, the requirement for them to be elected was removed, with coroners from this point onwards appointed by local authorities. The modern role of the coroner in Northern Ireland is detailed at **www.justice-ni.gov.uk/articles/coroners-service-northern-ireland**, and in the Republic at **www.citizensinformation.ie/en/death/sudden-or-unexplained-death/coroners/**.

Many coroners' records were destroyed during the Civil War, although some have survived from the nineteenth century, mainly from the 1880s, as well as fragmentary runs of additional coroners' returns included within official papers, which can provide summaries of findings, as can contemporary newspaper accounts of inquests. Following Partition, surviving coverage for the South is more extant, with access to records available at the NAI in Dublin. A useful description of holdings by archivist Brian Donnelly is included within an article entitled *Hospital Records in the National Archives of Ireland*, published in the Journal of the Irish Society for Archives, Winter 2008, and available online at **www.nationalarchives.ie/wp-content/uploads/2019/03/Hospital_records_BrianDonnelly.pdf**.

Dublin previously had two coroners' services, with courts for the Dublin City Coroner and the Dublin County Coroner, but these were merged in 2011, with cases now heard by the Dublin District Coroner's Court (**www.dublincoronerscourt.ie**). The NAI holds a substantial run of records for Dublin city from 1871 to 1933, with additional holdings up to 1984; after this copies of more recent records need to be requested from the Dublin District Coroner's Court via **dublincoroner@justice.ie**.

For Northern Ireland, PRONI holds over 25,000 coroners' inquest records from 1871 to 1999, although just over half of these relate to incidents from the Troubles of the late twentieth century (1969–1999). In the past, PRONI included an index to 6,206 sets of inquest papers from 1872 to 1920 within its online Name Search database, covering counties Antrim (1872–99), Armagh (1881–99), Down (1872–1920), Fermanagh (1887–1920), Londonderry (1891), Tyrone (1890–9), and Belfast (1894–1904); however, these were removed from the database in 2014, and are now searchable in the main catalogue, along with additional

CASE STUDY: From 16 to 18 March 1875, my four times great-uncle William Bill was tried at the assizes court in Belfast for the murder of his widowed cousin, 40-year-old Margaret Langtry, at Templepatrick, Co. Antrim, on Friday, 30 October 1874. The original trial papers have unfortunately not survived, but the case received extensive coverage in the Irish and British press.

At the hearing in the Crown Court of the county courthouse in Belfast, a jury heard how William regularly laboured for his uncle, David Bill, alongside his cousin, who worked as a housemaid, and who resided with David (also her uncle) along with her own three children. Tensions had come to a head between the cousins following the burial of a young sibling of William, 8-year-old Martha, just ten days earlier on 20 October 1874, with Margaret arguing that the lair used in the churchyard for Martha's burial was one that had been reserved for her. There were also further tensions concerning the land that David owned, which William's family hoped would come their way through inheritance at some point in the future; however, Margaret wanted David to sell his land, so that they could use the money to move to Belfast.

On the day of the murder, David had travelled into Belfast to pay his annual rent to the representatives of the Marquess of Donegal, and did not return to Templepatrick until late in the evening. Returning to his property, he noticed smoke coming from the kitchen door, and opened it to find the burning body of his niece lying before the fire. After quickly extinguishing the fire it soon became apparent that Margaret had been shot before her body had been set alight. A small sum of money was also discovered to have been stolen from a chest in an upstairs bedroom.

William had been absent for two days prior to the murder, and was soon arrested as the main suspect. On 11 November 1874 an inquest found that the cause of death was murder, and the proceedings were committed to a full trial – but not before a major revelation about William was revealed by the press. In 1869, he had previously been arrested for the murder of gentleman, by the name of William Courtenay. A subsequent trial, however, led to his being found not guilty when the jury could not agree on his culpability.

This was thus the second time that William was tried for murder. Each of his siblings gave evidence, as did his parents and his uncle, as well as others from the surrounding community, including officers of the law convinced of his guilt. After much deliberation, however, the jury once more returned a verdict of not-guilty, being unable to come up with a unanimous verdict, with many jurors citing a belief that some of the evidence was defective. As a consequence, William was once again absolved of the crime of a murder committed within the Templepatrick area, to the astonishment of many. Margaret Langtry's killer was never found.

In addition to the shock of the murder itself, the newspapers were able to provide an insight into the state of mind of William's mother, my four times great-grandmother Roseanna Bill (née Coulter), who was called to the stand, with the *Belfast News-Letter* recording her testimony. As noted, Roseanna's daughter (William's sister) Martha had died at the age of 8 on 20 October 1874, just ten days prior to the murder, and during her testimony she was reported to have stated the following:

> The prisoner is my son. He came home to me on Wednesday before he was arrested. I was in trouble about the death of my daughter … My son, the prisoner, was digging potatoes all day on Thursday, and he was also working on Friday. My husband went to Belfast about two o'clock on Friday morning, and did not come back to about eleven o'clock that night. I sat up for him, and all the rest were in bed when he arrived. In consequence of the trouble I was in about my daughter my appetite was very bad. Sometimes my appetite is so bad that I can hardly walk for weakness. William, the prisoner, went away up to snare rabbits. He took the snare [produced] with him. He came back with a rabbit. I skinned it, and soup was made of it. I took some of it, and the girls also got some. After he came home he sat down and took a smoke and then wound up his watch. It was twenty minutes to nine o'clock … I recollect my husband bringing ham and cheese the second night of my daughter's wake. It was rolled up in a piece of newspaper. The police searched the house, and abused it very badly. There is a man Wray (pointing to the sub-inspector) and I don't say he is a bad man, but he jeered and taunted at me.

(Belfast News-Letter (1875), *Assize News*. Thursday, 18 March. p.4 **www.britishnewspaperarchive.co.uk**: accessed 30 October 2024)

This summarised contribution of her testimony conveys so much about Roseanna's grief at the loss of her daughter, and the torment she was put through by the police when they came to arrest her son.

records up to 1999. For inquests after 1920, a Freedom of Information Act request is required to access such records (which can be made through its main enquiry service).

If seeking coroners' reports into events during the recent Troubles, PRONI has a guide available at **www.nidirect.gov.uk/articles/conflict-related-inquest-records**. Not all coroners' records are held by PRONI, with additional records held by the Coroners Service for Northern Ireland at Laganside House, 23–27 Oxford Street, Belfast, BT1 3LA, Tel: 0300 200 7811, email: **coronersoffice@courtsni.gov.uk**.

The death of a family member could also lead to economic opportunity for some within the family, with the subsequent inheritance of the deceased's estate. This in turn may have led to tensions and arguments within a family, sometimes even prior to the death of the individual concerned. The courts may have heard challenges to the inheritance of estates on many grounds, ranging from the diminished responsibility of a person writing a will prior to their death, to the wrong person succeeding in an inheritance.

A death may also have been the result of a deliberate attempt on someone's life, shattering the community within which it occurred. Murderers could expect to receive the death penalty in the Republic up to 1990, albeit for the killing of members of the Garda Síochána, prison officers and diplomats only, and in Northern Ireland up to 1973. (For more on those executed by the state for murder, see p.96.)

In some cases the murder of an individual may have been due to internal family strife, an allegation that was certainly asserted within the Bill case study, revealing a great deal about an internal family rift.

Suicide

Suicide ceased to be a crime in Northern Ireland in 1966, following the Criminal Justice Act (Northern Ireland), and in the Republic in 1993, following the Criminal Law (Suicide) Act. In both jurisdictions, aiding and abetting a suicide continues to be a felony, punishable by up to fourteen years' imprisonment.

A person who committed suicide was historically termed 'felo de se' in legal terms. In many cases, attempts at suicide followed mental or physical deterioration, while drink was often a common catalyst. Historically, while the deceased could not be prosecuted for the crime of suicide, his or her estate could be forfeited to the Crown prior to 1870.

Such was the stigma of suicide that victims were buried at a crossroads, not in consecrated ground, and with a stake driven through the body, although this practice ended in July 1823 following parliamentary

CASE STUDY: One of the earliest cases from the PRONI records is that of a soldier called Robert Courtney, who attempted to kill himself in late October 1900, as recorded by the *Irish News and Belfast Morning News*:

> On the evening of the 30th ult. Robert Courtney, an army pensioner, aged 68, attempted to commit suicide by cutting his throat at Glynn, near Larne. Fortunately the knife was not sharp, and his wife succeeded in wresting it from him before he had done himself serious injury. He was removed yesterday morning to the Larne Union Hospital, where Dr Killen discovered he had severed several veins on the left side of the neck, but it is not anticipated the wound will prove serious.
>
> (*Irish News and Belfast Morning News* (1900). Attempted Suicide Near Larne. Thursday, 1 November. p.2. **www.britishnewspaperarchive.co.uk**: accessed 30 October 2024)

Further press reports note that due to ill health the trial of Courtney was postponed on a few occasions. In June 1901, the same newspaper reported the following:

> Mr Carr made a further application for the adjournment in the case of Robert Courtney, who was charged with having attempted to commit suicide. Accused, who was an old pensioner, was still unable to appear owing to the serious nature of the injuries he had inflicted.
>
> Mr Harper, on behalf of the accused, received a certificate from Lieutenant-Colonel McFarland MD, stating that the accused had been 2 years on the recruiting staff at Belfast. He had served a long period on foreign service, and had had a sunstroke, since which he had been subject to melancholia. He had made an attempt since, and had been in a feeble state of health, and was unfit to take his trial. A sad feature in connection with the man's family was that his son had been drowned at Malta, and his only daughter killed in a railway accident, while another son, who was in the Grenadier Guards, had been invalided home from South Africa. Mr Harper said that he feared the continuous adjournment of the case was having a most retarding effect upon the old man's mind and state of health.

> Mr Carr urged that the difficulty was to protect the accused against himself. He had spoken to the surgeon, who would not take the responsibility of saying it would be safe to allow the old man his liberty. The wife of Courtney would not take the responsibility of watching him.
>
> The case was again adjourned.
>
> (*Irish News and Belfast Morning News* (1901). Application for Adjournment. Friday, 21 June. p.6. **www.britishnewspaper archive.co.uk**: accessed 30 October 2024)

PRONI holds records from Courtney's subsequent trial under ANT/1/1/B/1/13/9, dated 25 April 1902. These papers add considerably more detail than the newspaper coverage, as they include witness statements from those who found Courtney after his suicide attempt. His wife Margaret noted in her statement:

> On that morning I noticed that he seemed ill and tired. He went out to the garden and came back about one o'clock. He came in and sat a moment at the fire and got up and went out again. I shortly after went out to look for him. About 6 o'clock that evening I heard moans coming from the hay loft. My daughter Margaret Courtney and myself went out with a candle and searched the hay loft, and found my husband lying in the hay loft, among the hay. He was unconscious. I saw some blood on on his collar. I did not examine closer at that time. I sent at once for the doctor.

When cross-examined, she further added that 'He was at times depressed. A daughter since dead was unwell at that time. He was more depressed than usual on that account.'

The medical practitioner who found him, William James Wilson of Larne, told the court:

> I found him in the hay loft at the rear of his house. I found an incised wound on his throat three inches long. It went into the wind pipe. I considered his life in danger. He was unconscious then. I dressed the wound and had him removed to Larne Workhouse Infirmary. He recovered consciousness at his own house while in the hay loft. In my opinion this wound would

> have caused death if he had not been treated. In my opinion the wound was self-inflicted.
>
> Again, following a cross-examination, Wilson added: 'In my opinion the prisoner was not accountable for his actions. I had not treated him before this.'
>
> Courtney was not convicted. He eventually passed away at 57 Cedar Avenue, Belfast, on 6 March 1905, the cause of death being rheumatism and exhaustion.

intervention which made it illegal. From 1824 to 1870 suicides were to be buried in a churchyard at night between 9 p.m. and midnight, with no Christian rituals performed, but in 1882 the Interments (felo de se) Act permitted suicide victims to be buried in a graveyard at any hour, and with full Christian rites.

Quarter session records for individual attempted suicide cases, including charge sheets, are available at PRONI, catalogued for the courts at Belfast, Antrim, Armagh and Down, although there is an access closure policy in place for records from the most recent one hundred years. The earliest surviving record is from 12 January 1893. Some of the cases are name searchable on the catalogue, others merely list the date and the words 'named individual – attempted suicide'. By contrast, very few records are available through the online NAI catalogue.

Prior to 1824, those who committed suicide were not permitted to be buried in a church graveyard.

Chapter 3

LAW AND ORDER

Everybody in Ireland had to live within the law, but at various points in history the question of whose law should be obeyed was one that often led to conflict. From the early Brehon laws to the imposition of English law, to the recent Troubles of the early and latter parts of the twentieth century, many people suffered as victims of crimes or civil injuries. Others were prosecuted in the pursuit of justice, and made to pay a price in restitution, whether through a fine, imprisonment, transportation, or even death.

In this chapter I will explain how the law of the land existed historically in Ireland, and provide some examples of records that may help to place our ancestors into various judicial landscapes. This is unfortunately one area where Ireland's documentary records have been severely impacted by the events of 1922, and the destruction of the Four Courts in Dublin, the very name of which should provide a clue as to why. Again however, the glass is not quite empty – there are many sources that can still assist us in researching our ancestral crises when it comes to the law, not least of which the newspaper coverage of the last 200 years and more.

The Brehon Laws
Early Ireland was a tribal society, with inhabitants living within large kin groups known as 'fine', sub-divided into smaller family groupings known in Gaelic as 'dearbhfhine', with members sharing descent from a common great-grandfather. Although never part of a unified nation, these early Irish inhabitants did share the same culture and Gaelic language, and adhered to a civil legal system known as the Brehon laws (from Irish 'brethim', meaning 'judge'), dating back to at least the fifth century AD, and lasting for more than a thousand years. Originally preserved orally, many of the laws were transcribed, with the eighth century Senchus Mór just one collection documented from the period.

Through the Brehon laws system, criminal affronts were solved through the use of arbitration and compensation. With both parties to a dispute agreeing in advance to abide by a given verdict, skilled advocates would then present their cases to an independent judge. If the judge found in the victim's favour, the victim was due compensation to the satisfaction of his 'honour price', known in Irish as his 'lóg n-enech' (the 'price of his face'), the level of which depended on his status in society; in the case of a murder, this compensation was complemented with a further payment known in Irish as the 'éraic', or 'body fine', made to the wider dearbhfhine, which was the equivalent of the deceased's honour price. If the offender was unable to pay the fines imposed, his kin group would be liable to make the payment, and the plaintiff could seize property from a kin member to force payment (known as the 'distraint' process); if there were no surviving family members to take up the burden, the guilty party could be enslaved or put to death. If the guilty party breached the agreement to honour a verdict and refused to pay the compensation, he could be ostracised from his family grouping and the wider society around him.

On civil matters, most contracts entered into between two parties came with a surety clause, with a guarantor known as a 'ráth' offering a guarantee that the terms of a contract would be fulfilled, upon pain of forfeiture of his own property. An agreement could not be entered into at a level higher than a person's honour price.

The Brehon laws also had a major influence on the regulation of property and inheritance, with its laws of succession codified through the rules of 'tanistry' ('tanaisteacht' in Irish). Through these, a king or chief known as a 'toisech' would be succeeded by a deputy known as a 'tanist'. Early Irish society did not exercise primogeniture, and so the tanist, who had previously been elected from close relatives within the dearbhfhine, was not necessarily a son of the present incumbent. From these ancient roles come the modern political offices in Ireland of Taoiseach, the Irish Prime Minister, and Tánaiste, the Deputy Prime Minister.

Women are often noted as having certain freedoms according to the Brehon laws, although only to a certain extent. For example, although a man had a right to 'correct' (beat) his wife, if he struck her so hard that a visible mark was left, the wife could seek a divorce; similarly, if he was impotent, the wife could also seek to leave her marriage. However, women were still deemed to be of much lower status than men, with offences against them normally treated as offences against their guardians.

Brehon Law officially ceased to offer a legal form of address from 1603, following a decree from James I of Britain that all Irish subjects were now under the king's protection, and subject to English law.

For more on the Brehon Laws read Fergus Kelly's *A Guide to Early Irish Law* (Dublin Institute for Advanced Studies, 1988).

English Law

From the twelfth century, English law began to make inroads into Ireland, and to compete with the Brehon Laws system in areas that fell to the Crown. In 1210, King John decreed that English law was to be adhered to in his lordship of Ireland. Over the following two centuries efforts were made to track Irish common law with English common law, while various statutes drawn up in England were also directly imposed on Ireland – or at least on the parts of the island that fell under the control or influence of the Crown, mainly in Dublin, Louth, Meath and Kildare.

From the early fourteenth century the English lordship began to decline, with many of the Anglo-Norman colonists, who later became known to history as the 'Old English', intermarrying with local Irish Gaelic families; in adopting their traditions and language, they became a hybrid nation said to be 'more Irish than the Irish'. To counter this, in 1366 the Statues of Kilkenny were passed by the Irish Parliament, which

Reginald's Tower, Ireland's oldest civic building, was built by the Anglo-Normans after their conquest of Waterford.

dictated that those living within Dublin's Pale, and other areas of English influence, had to speak the English language, adopt English names, to use English law to resolve disputes, and to prevent intermarriage with local Irish Gaelic families. This legislation was not formally repealed in the Republic until the Statute Law Revision Act of 1983. To further curb the power of the Old English, in 1494 Poynings' Law was passed which decreed that any bills passing through the Irish Parliament had to be signed off in England by the king and his privy council. This measure continued until its abolition in 1782, although the independence gained by the Irish Parliament at this point was brief, with its subsequent abolition just eighteen years later, thanks to the Act of Union with Britain in 1800.

A major turning point for the wider adoption of English law in Ireland was during the mid to late sixteenth century, when many Irish lords were forced to surrender their lands and to have them regranted to them by the Crown. Following the English Reformation of the 1530s, a series of carefully planned colonial 'plantations', or colonies, were also attempted in Ireland by the Crown, in counties Laois and Offaly, in Munster, and then from 1609 across much of Ulster (p.124), further extending the Crown's reach and the rule of English law, which soon gained primacy.

The Crown Courts

The courts system in Ireland, adhering initially to English law, at first replicated much of what was happening in England itself, and in the late medieval period evolved into what became known as the 'Four Courts'. The term may be familiar, in that it was the bombardment of the Four Courts in Dublin in 1922 that led to the destruction of Ireland's Public Record Office, and eight centuries worth of Ireland's documented history, including its court records. However, some records have survived, mainly through surrogate copies held elsewhere, most notably at the National Archives of the UK. The job of the Four Courts was to interpret the laws of the English, Irish and British Parliaments, as pertaining to Ireland.

The first centralised civil court, the King's Court, was established in the late twelfth century, and heard cases across the lordship, as well as in Dublin; by the late thirteenth century it had evolved into the Court of Common Pleas, which heard civil cases between Irish citizens, both in Dublin (and temporarily in Carlow, for thirty years beginning in the 1360s) and through local assizes. Nothing has survived from this court prior to the late eighteenth century.

The Court of the King's Bench, was the most senior court to hear both criminal and civil processes. It emerged in the late fourteenth century, and took up a permanent holding in Dublin from the sixteenth century, where it would hear criminal cases that disturbed the 'King's Peace'. From 1729 onwards, serious cases that had previously been heard by the Court of the King's Bench were now to be heard by the new Dublin Commission Court.

Elsewhere in the country, judges of the Court of the King's Bench would travel on regular geographical circuits known as 'assizes', on the authority of what were known as commissions of 'oyer and terminer' (meaning 'to hear and determine'), as granted by the Crown. This gave them the authority to determine which felonies and misdemeanours had been carried out within their particular jurisdictions, and to hear the most serious civil and criminal cases, as well as cases referred to them from the quarter sessions. The assize court system started initially in the medieval period through a series of local circuits known as 'eyres', with the last of these carried out in the fourteenth century. By the early seventeenth century, in the aftermath of the Flight of the Earls of 1607, Gaelic resistance to English law had been all but crushed, making it considerably easier to now fully implement a more complete nationwide system. From this point there were five geographic assizes circuits in operation, on which judges would hear cases from each county in turn; from 1796 to 1850 this was expanded to six circuits. From 1695 there were two visits carried out per year, but by 1877 this was changed to a simple winter assize for each province, with most civil cases by this point now being handled by the quarter sessions in a county court.

Prior to an assize hearing, prisoners would have first been brought before a justice of the peace or magistrate at a petty sessions court (p.81) to decide if the case was serious enough to be referred to the assizes; if so, the case would be referred to the grand jury (p.83), which would issue the indictment. Prisoners would then be held on remand, potentially for months awaiting the arrival of the judge and for the assize court to be convened.

The medieval Chancery system was created in 1232, and by 1534 had become the third of the Four Courts based in the capital, in time hearing inheritance cases and cases of bankruptcy, particularly following the Famine with its involvement in administering the Encumbered Estates Acts (see p.133). While all of its records were destroyed in 1922, the 'Calendar of Irish Chancery Letters c.1244–1509' project, aka 'CIRCLE 2.0', is presented on the Virtual Treasury of Ireland platform as a gold seam at **https://virtualtreasury.ie/gold-seams/circle**. This comprises over 15,000 Chancery letters from the period, translated into English, and includes source material from the National Library of Ireland, Dublin City Library and Archives, the Irish Record Commission, the National Archives of Ireland, the UK National Archives, and the Huntingdon Library in California, USA.

The Court of Exchequer was the fourth of the Four Courts, responsible for collecting the king's revenue (from rents, fines and customs duties) and for government expenditure issues, as well as debt issues to the Crown. The Virtual Record Treasury of Ireland hosts another gold seam entitled 'Medieval Exchequer: thirteenth–fifteenth centuries' available to consult at **https://virtualtreasury.ie/gold-seams/medieval-exchequer**, populated with surrogate copies of the exchequer records from 1250 to 1450. These exist thanks to the corruption of the early Irish exchequer, which was often accused of theft from the king and for maladministration of the finances. So bad was its reputation that from the late thirteenth century the Crown required all Irish exchequer accounts to be signed off by the king's clerks at Westminster, and thus a copy of the records was created, which survived the 1922 fire in Dublin, and which are held at the UK National Archives, catalogued under E 101. In addition to this, two parchment memoranda rolls from the fourteenth century actually survived the blaze in Dublin, while fifty additional rolls were transcribed by the Irish Manuscript Commission in the nineteenth century, all of which are included. In addition to digitised images of the originals, calendars have also been digitised summarising the records from 1270 to 1449, as created by Dr Philomena Connolly.

Following the Supreme Court of Judicature Act (Ireland) Act of 1877, the Four Courts were merged to create the Supreme Court of Judicature, which comprised a new High Court of Justice and a separate Court of Appeal. Following the Government of Ireland Act of 1920, the Supreme Court was abolished, with the High Court split into new courts for Northern Ireland and Southern Ireland, alongside a split Appeals Court. The High Court of the South was replaced in 1924 by a new High Court of the Irish Free State, while the Northern High Court continued.

Surviving courts' material held at the National Archives of Ireland are unfortunately not searchable through its online catalogue, but a detailed guide summarising what is available is located at **www.nationalarchives.ie/legal-records/court-records-held-in-the-national-archives/**. Finding aids for records from the individual courts can be consulted in the Reading Room.

In addition, some records' sets have been digitised by FamilySearch and commercial genealogy companies, with a useful list available at **www.familysearch.org/en/wiki/Ireland_Court_Records**.

> **TIP:** For legislation that has been passed by the Irish Parliament prior to its abolition in 1800, John Levin's Statutes Project blog at **https://statutes.org.uk/site/collections/british-and-irish/ireland-to-1800/** provides links to published volumes held at the *Oireachtas* Library and other sources. Queen's University Belfast also has a useful Irish legislation database at **www.qub.ac.uk/ild/**, which can be searched by keyword.
>
> Acts of Parliament passed through the Westminster Parliament are detailed at **www.legislation.gov.uk**, while for the post-1922 Free State, and later the Republic, legislation is documented at **www.irishstatutebook.ie** (including some pre-1922 statutes). For acts of the Northern Irish Parliament from 1922 to 1971, visit **www.legislation.gov.uk/apni**.
>
> The Stormont debates archive for Northern Ireland is available at **https://web.archive.org/web/20120516083736/http://stormontpapers.ahds.ac.uk/index.html**, while the UK parliamentary record is available via Hansard at **https://hansard.parliament.uk**. The UK Parliamentary Papers website at **https://parlipapers.proquest.com/parlipapers**, unfortunately accessible only via institutional subscription at archives and libraries, also carries additional papers from 1714 to 1911.

Local Courts

In addition to the Four Courts, which heard the most serious cases, minor offences, both criminal and civil, could be heard at a local level through quarter sessions and petty sessions.

From 1415 justices of the peace were magistrates empowered in Ireland to hold 'quarter sessions' in which more minor civil and criminal cases could be heard, either dispensing justice summarily, without a trial, or by referring more serious cases to the grand jury, to be prepared for the next assize court. Drawn largely from the gentry, although with some clergymen also in post, justices of the peace were not legally trained or paid, and many did not fulfil their duties.

It was not until the seventeenth century that there was a more prolific nationwide system for the magistrates to administer justice. From the nineteenth century the justices also dealt with less serious crimes outwith

> **CASE STUDY:** On 16 May 1861, a member of my extended family in County Donegal, Robert Strain, from Tullyvinny townland in the parish of Raphoe, appeared as the plaintiff at the petty sessions court at Raphoe to accuse Thomas Shaw of Coolaghy of trespass, seeking damages of £1 10s.
>
> Following the hearing, the justice of the peace summarily ordered Shaw to pay the damages sought. At the same time Shaw had planned to counter-sue Strain, accusing him of being 'malicious', and 'turning Phipps' cattle into Phipps' stock yard on the 10th Octr last'.
>
> However, having already been found guilty by the magistrate, the second case was not heard, with the final column in the record stating simply 'no appearance'.
>
> (Ireland, Petty Session Court Registers. 16 May 1861. Robert Strain, defendant. **www.findmypast.ie**: accessed 30 October 2024)

the bounds of the quarter sessions, through what were known as the 'petty sessions'. Each trial had no jury in attendance, and was presided over by a magistrate or two justices of the peace.

It should be noted that from June 1920 to early 1923, during the War of Independence and at the start of the subsequent Civil War, a series of non-British republican courts were briefly established by the Dáil government to try to undermine the legitimacy of British rule in Ireland. Known as the 'Dáil courts' or 'Sinn Féin courts', they were courts of arbitration, with any judgments concluded enforced by the IRA and the Irish Republican Police. Following the emergence of the Irish Free State in December 1922, the work of the courts was finally disestablished through the Dáil Éireann Courts (Winding Up) Act 1923.

Records from the petty sessions courts and quarter sessions for the Republic of Ireland are held at the NAI, with a guide available at **www.nationalarchives.ie/article/guide-court-records-ireland-pre-1922/**. The petty sessions records, comprising some 11,000 books documenting more than 22 million cases, have been digitised and made available through Findmypast's 'Ireland, Petty Sessions Court Registers', covering the period from 1851 to 1924, however, there are gaps in the records, particularly for Dublin. The available coverage is listed at **www.findmypast.ie/articles/irish-petty-sessions-order-books**. After 1924 the system was changed, with the petty sessions and quarters sessions being reconstituted as district courts.

Larne Courthouse in County Antrim dispensed local justice from 1903 to 2013, when it was eventually closed down by the courts' service.

In Northern Ireland, the petty sessions court system continued until 1978, with records held at PRONI, catalogued from HA/1/1 to HA/1/117 ('Records of the Petty Sessions Courts'), although a search under the term 'petty sessions' on the PRONI calendar will also reveal individual papers from other sources concerned with the courts. There is unfortunately no guide to the court records held at PRONI on its website, save for a brief mention on the Family and Local History Records guide at **www.nidirect.gov.uk/articles/family-and-local-history-records**.

Quarter sessions records for Northern Ireland are catalogued by county, dating back to 1822 for Antrim (ANT/1/1), 1875 for Armagh (ARM/1/1), 1893 for Down (DOW/1/1), 1871 for Fermanagh (FER/1/1), 1895 for Londonderry (LON/1/1), and 1877 for Tyrone (TYR/1/1).

Grand Juries

From Anglo-Norman times until the introduction of county councils in 1898, 'grand juries' acted as the main administrative arm of local government, meeting twice a year at the spring and autumn assizes, and at 'quarter sessions' four times a year.

Grand juries were tasked not only with judicial functions, but with facilitating public works in their locales, such as road and bridge repairs, the maintenance of gaols and hospitals, and setting local taxes such as the county cess. They were made up of between twelve and twenty-three volunteer jurors, and appointed by the High Sheriff for the county mainly from the landlord class (but not from the aristocracy), with Roman Catholics excluded from membership until 1793. Much of the communications' infrastructure of Ireland exists today as a result of their early efforts, but being drawn largely from the landlord class, the juries were deeply unpopular in parts of the country.

The administrative powers of grand juries were stripped away from 1898, but they continued to meet at the assizes in a judicial capacity. Following Partition in 1922 they were abolished altogether in the Free State, but continued to meet in Northern Ireland until their eventual abolition in 1969.

Grand jury records are available in many archives, with some collections online, including the 'Donegal, Grand Jury Presentments 1753–1899' collection on Findmypast, and the 'Louth Grand Jury Query Books (1786–1813, 1815–1816, 1823–1899)' collection on the Louth County Archives Service website at **www.louthcoco.ie/en/services/archives**.

A detailed list of surviving grand jury records for Ulster's nine counties is included in William Roulston's book (p.12). Further information on the records can also be found in *People, Place and Power: The Grand Jury System in Ireland* (Brian Gurrin & others, Trinity College Dublin, 2021), which can be found on the Virtual Record Treasury of Ireland platform at **https://beyond2022.ie/the-grand-jury-system-in-ireland**.

Manor Records

During the plantations of the seventeenth century, the manorial system was revived as a means to help administer estates in Ireland, with the re-establishment of manorial courts, which had previously existed during the period of the early Anglo-Norman lordship. Although not many records have survived for the majority of the country, in the areas where they do they can be particularly useful for research. A parliamentary enquiry in 1837 noted the existence at that stage of some 204 such courts in Ireland, with over half in Ulster and a quarter in Munster, although by now most were acting almost exclusively in the capacity of small debts courts. Manorial courts were formally abolished in Ireland in 1857.

In 1604, the Earl of Antrim, Randal MacDonnell, was granted a charter in 1604 to hold manorial courts on his lands, and duly established four in the four lower baronies of his estates in the north of Antrim, which were located in his manors at Ballycastle, Dunluce, Glenarm and Oldstone. The 'court leet' (also termed 'a view of frankpledge') was originally

CASE STUDY: The following three examples from the Manor Court Book of Caledon Estate, in Counties Tyrone and Armagh, show the range of civil complaints that could be heard by the court leet and court baron.

The first concerns a simple matter of debt, heard on Monday, 4 November 1839 at Caledon, with Alexander Pringle acting as foreman of the jury:

> No. 9. Patrick Hughes of Ahemis, Farmer @ James McShane of Caledon, Labourer
>
> £1:15:0 being the rem[ainde]r of a larger sum due by the Def[endan]t to Pl[aintif]f on a settled act
>
> Patrick Hughes sworn proves that the Def[endan]ts acknowledgment of £2:5:0 and that he allowed 10 shillings to Def[endan]t for manure reducing the debt to £1:15:0.
>
> Decree for full amount for self & fellows
>
> Alexander Pringle
>
> (Manorial registers. 4 November 1839. Manor Court Book, Caledon Estate, at Co. Tyrone and Armagh, Ireland (1839–1859). D266/336. PRONI, Belfast)

The following comes from the same court held at Caledon on Monday, 2 March 1840, with James Keenan acting as the jury foreman. It concerns a quarrel over an apprenticeship that was never completed:

> No. 2. James Carroll of Curfeighan @ Michael Hughes of Unchog, Tailor
>
> £1.16.11 being a sum paid as a Fee by Pl[aintif]f to Def[endan]t for Def[endan]ts learning Pl[aintif]fs Son the Trade of Tailor which Trade Def[endan]t did not give Pl[aintif]fs Son & which sum Pl[aintif]f reasonably deserves to have & recover from Def[endan]t.

> Plaintiff sworn – proves the advance of £2:0:0 to Def[endan]t an act of getting his son a trade from said Def[endan]t – was to serve Def[endan]t 5 years but no Indenture.
>
> Defence – Mich[ae]l McKenna a sworn proves the willingness of Def[endan]t to teach Pat[ric]k Carrol a trade but Carroll left Def[endan]ts employment.
>
> A dismiss for self and fellows.
>
> James Keenan
>
> (Ibid. 2 March 1840)

On the same day the court heard a quarrel about a debt, although in this case the plaintiff himself was not squeaky clean!

> No. 3. Mr John Hall of Mullamossagh vs. Cornelius Reilly of Caledon
>
> £1:10:0 added to Pl[aintif]fs years rent by Def[endan]t over and above the sum of £13:18:1 which was Pl[aintif]fs rent in the year 1832, which was fraudulently returned in Def[endant]s report in the year 1836, when Pl[aintif]f was in the Gaol of Armagh.
>
> No evidence produced on the part of the Plaintiff
>
> A dismiss for self and fellows.
>
> James Keenan
>
> (Ibid. 2 March 1840)

a criminal court made up of a jury of freeholders which heard petty common law offences, but its role was soon taken over by the role of magistrates, leaving it with purely administrative functions. The 'court baron' handled civil cases, such as cases involving debts, with its work later subsumed into a new 'court of record', established from 1629, which could hear claims up to the value of £10. In charge of the courts was an appointed judicial officer known as a 'seneschal'.

The earlier responsibilities of these courts also included the registrations of deeds and leases, although the nature of cases later heard became more petty, as a civil court structure began to emerge in the counties. The earliest surviving records from the courts date to 1742, and are held at PRONI under D/2977. An article by Ian Montgomery in the Ulster Historical Foundation's *Familia* publication from 2000 (Number 16) gives a comprehensive overview of the areas that they covered.

The Manor Courts of the Earl of Thomond 1666–1686 by S.C. O'Mahony, published in 2004 within *Analecta Hibernica* (2004, No. 38, pp.135, 137–220), provides a detailed overview of the work in the Earl of Thomond's estates within County Clare. In the work of the courts, O'Mahony notes that 'All of society is there: Esquires, gentlemen, merchants, tradesmen, farmers, labourers, with Gael and Gall at every level.' The source for the material published is found in a manuscript within the Petworth Papers of the Earls of Egremont, as held at West Sussex Record Office in Chichester, England (catalogued as Ms C 10/7), providing a good example that not all records concerning Ireland may necessarily be found in Ireland. It includes material for the West Clare manors of Crovraghan, Kilrush, Moigh, Finavarra, Innish and Clonrond, Bunratty, Doonass and Castlebank, as well as for Fedamore in County Limerick and Cullen in County Tipperary.

Elsewhere, Raymond Gillespie's article 'A Manor Court in Seventeenth Century Ireland' in *Irish Economic and Social History* (1998, Vol. 25, pp.81–87) cites many further examples of the work of manorial courts in Limerick, Dublin, Cork and Counties Antrim, Armagh, Clare and Kilkenny.

Church Courts

From 1537 the Protestant based Church of Ireland, aka the Anglican or Episcopal church, was the state church, a role it fulfilled until its eventual disestablishment in January 1871. Following disestablishment its records were deemed to be state records, and were thus transferred to the Public Record Office in Dublin, an unfortunate act in hindsight that led to their later destruction in the 1922 fire. Among the records destroyed were those from the church's courts, although some holdings have survived in original or surrogate form. The courts dealt with a range of issues, including marriage law prior to 1844, marital separations (p.56), and probate cases.

> **CASE STUDY**: Some of the most common cases heard by the various Presbyterian kirk sessions were those involving pre-marital sex, recorded as 'antenuptial fornication' in the jargon of the day, as typified by the following examples from County Antrim:
>
> 3 August 1862
>
> The Session met and was constituted by Mr Black Elders present John Gibson, James Gibson, and Samuel Wallace.
>
> Margaret Bell appeared to express her sorrow & contrition for the sin of fornication and after being suitably admonished by the Moderator she was returned to the enjoyment of church privileges.
>
> James Black
> Samuel Wilson, Clerk
>
> (Kirk sessions. Ireland. Presbyterian Lylehill, Templepatrick, Co. Antrim. 3 August 1862. BELL, Margaret. MIC 1P/98. PRONI, Belfast)
>
> 23 May 1872
>
> The Session met at Dunamargy (Dunamuggy) on fast day, and after being regularly constituted. Present, James Keir, John Gavin, and Rev Joseph McKee, Moderator.
>
> Margaret Jameson (otherwise Davidson) appeared before them to give satisfaction for the sin of antenuptial fornication and after expressing sorrow for her sin against God and the Laws of the Church she was duly restored to Privilege of the Church.
>
> (Kirk sessions. Ireland. Presbyterian 2nd Donegore, Co. Antrim. 23 May 1872. JAMESON, Margaret. MIC 1P 153/1–2. PRONI, Belfast)

Probate matters prior to 1858 were handled by a series of Anglican consistorial courts which existed for each diocese. Among the records that have survived are will books for Down, 1850–58, and for Connor, 1818–20 and 1853–58, which can be found online at **http://census.nationalarchives.ie/search/dw/home.jsp**. The same database also hosts surviving will books from the higher Prerogative Court, which heard cases for larger estates, with coverage available for the years 1664–84, 1706–8, 1726–8, 1728–9, 1777, 1813, and 1834. Grant books for the dioceses of Cashel (1840–5), Derry and Raphoe (1812–51) and Ossory (1848–58), have also survived and can be consulted at the NAI. A detailed guide to additional holdings can be found on John Grenham's site at **www.johngrenham.com/browse/retrieve_text.php?text_contentid=523**.

Church of Ireland parishes each had their own vestries, which handled a range of daily activities including the election of wardens (two per parish, and not necessarily members of the Anglican Church), the setting of the parish cess, oversight of the parochial road network, the administration of poor relief, the setting and collection of tithes, and more. A guide to help locate surviving vestry records at the Representative Church Body Library in Dublin is available at **www.ireland.anglican.org/about/rcb-library/online-parish-records**, while the PRONI Guide to Church Records can also advise on material available at PRONI in Belfast at **www.nidirect.gov.uk/publications/proni-guide-church-records**.

For the Presbyterian churches, the lowest of the church courts was the kirk session, which could try its parishioners for breaches of discipline. Surviving session registers can be found at PRONI and the Presbyterian Historical Society of Ireland in Belfast, and are again documented in the PRONI Guide to Church Records.

Police and Prison Records

The organisation of a modern police force in Ireland started in 1816 with the creation of the Peace Preservation Force, followed by the establishment of individual county constabularies in 1822. In 1836 the Dublin Metropolitan Police was founded to replace the city's county constabulary, with the same year also seeing the creation of the national Irish Constabulary, later to become the Royal Irish Constabulary (RIC), which continued as the main police force across the island until the Partition of Ireland. In the Free State from 1922 the RIC was replaced by An Garda Síochána, while in Northern Ireland the Royal Ulster Constabulary was created, which later gave way in 2001 to the Police Service of Northern Ireland.

RIC service records are held at the UK's National Archives, but have been digitised and made available on Findmypast. Collections available include 'Ireland, Royal Irish Constabulary Service Records 1816–1922', 'Ireland, Royal Irish Constabulary Pensions 1826–1925', and 'Ireland, Royal Irish Constabulary History & Directories'. The latter includes six different publications printed between 1871 and 1920, and sixty-eight

Records for the Royal Irish Constabulary, and for the British administration operating from Dublin Castle are held at the UK National Archives at Kew, near London.

pieces from the archive's HO 184 collection. Findmypast also hosts the 'Ireland, Dublin Metropolitan Police General Register 1837–1925' collection, noting recruitment and transfers within the force, as well as a third party index, 'Ireland, Dublin Metropolitan Police Prisoners Books 1905–1908 and 1911–1918', indexing the Dublin Metropolitan Police's Prisoners Books from 1911 to 1918. These can also be freely viewed online at **https://digital.ucd.ie/view/ucdlib:43945**, with each volume including a name index. Among the high profile arrests documented within this period are James Connolly and James Larkin on 30 and 31 August 1913 (p.227, Book 3, 1911–1913), with the charge for both being 'incitement to crime', as part of the events surrounding the Dublin Lockout (p.138).

The history section of An Garda Síochána's site at **www.garda.ie/en/About-Us/Our-History** includes a Roll of Honour for all those who have lost their lives in service since 1922, information about the holdings of the Garda Museum at Dublin Castle, recipients of the Scott Medal (the Garda's highest award), and on the Garda's archives. If you wish to locate service information for ancestors, you will need to contact the museum, but the holdings are quite limited, in the form of service record extracts. Only those who served, or their family members, can gain access. Many of the original service records prior to the 1950s have not survived, but the museum has previously advised me that those that have cannot be consulted anyway, only the extracts.

The Police Service of Northern Ireland (PSNI) website at **www.psni.police.uk** includes an 'Our History' section within the site's 'About Us' section. This has a Police Museum, and a 'Genealogy' section, with details on searches that it can provide into RIC service records from 1822 to 1922, as well as from various printed RIC lists held at the museum. For service within the later RUC, the current PSNI museum has a series of service record cards that continue up to 1977, after which they have been computerised. A similar set-up exists for records of the PSNI itself, which replaced the RUC in 2001. There is a seventy-five-year closure period for access to these cards by the general public, although ex-policemen or their family members can view more recent records if the relevant proof of relationship to the officer concerned is supplied. Contact the museum by email via the details given on the site.

Several online resources can help to determine if your ancestor was ever on the wrong side of the law. Editions of *The Police Gazette or Hue and Cry* can be found in Ancestry's 'Ireland, Police Gazettes, 1861–1893' collection, with information on wanted criminals, crimes committed, criminals who had been apprehended, and missing persons. Issues from 1863 to 1893 can also be accessed at the pay-per-view Last Chance to Read, at **www.lastchancetoread.com**, while some later editions from 1915 to 1922 can be found also at the Oireachtas Library website (p.16).

Crumlin Road Gaol, Belfast.

Kilmainham Gaol, Dublin.

Findmypast's 'Ireland, Outrage Reports 1836–1840' further describes incidents recorded by the RIC.

Findmypast's 'Irish Prison Registers 1790–1924' collection, also sourced from the NAI, contains over 3.5 million entries covering imprisonment of prisoners within various custodial institutions, including bridewells, county prisons and sanatoriums for alcoholics. Most records provide details such as name of the prisoner, address, place of birth, occupation, religion, education, age, physical description, name and address of next of kin, the crime committed, sentence, dates of committal and release/decease. The most common offence recorded was drunkenness, followed by theft and assault. The collection is again not comprehensive, with some local registers still held in private hands, and records for Northern Ireland are not included.

The same collection is hosted on FamilySearch (within the 'United Kingdom and Ireland' category). The returned index details are more limited, providing the person's name and role (e.g. prisoner), the year of the event and where it happened, age, birthplace and year of birth, brief details of the offence and the relevant accession number for the record.

There is not a great deal of Irish material on MyHeritage, but it does included an 'Irish Prisoners 1780–1867' database. Going further back, Eddie Connolly has transcribed an 1853 publication of the Ulster Roll of

> **CASE STUDY:** A typical case study found within the Findmypast Irish Prison Registers 1790–1924 collection concerns a young Roman Catholic labourer called Michael Ryan from Bray, who was committed to Kilmainham Gaol on 8 April 1885.
>
> The record notes that Ryan was just 18 years of age, was 5ft 10in tall, and with brown hair, hazel eyes, and a fresh skin complexion. He weighed 157 pounds, and could read and write. The record also notes that he had various tattoos on his left arm, with 'N.R.' inscribed alongside an image of an anchor and a dot, while he was also noted to have a mark on his breast and another on the right side of his nose. His crime was 'larceny from person', and he was sentenced by Mr Justice Johnston on the same day to seven calendar months with hard labour. The sentence was due to expire on 7 November 1885, but a note in the margin states that he was sent to Richmond Lunatic Asylum on 6 May.
>
> (Dublin-Kilmainham Prison General Register 1883–1888, Bk no. 1/10/18; RYAN, Michael, 8 April 1885. Irish Prison Registers 1790–1924, **Findmypast.co.uk**: accessed 30 October 2024)

Gaol Delivery, 1613–18, starting at **http://anextractofreflection.blogspot.com/2013/09/ulster-roll-of-gaol-delivery-1613–1618.html**.

Newspaper collections (p.22) are also well worth consulting for reportage of crimes, investigations and eventual proceedings if a case went to trial, while the catalogues of both PRONI and the NAI should be examined.

Many Irish folk who migrated to Britain found themselves on the wrong side of the law, particularly because of the harsh anti-Catholic laws and the rise of republicanism as a political movement throughout the nineteenth century. The Old Bailey Online website, which carries the proceedings of the Central Criminal Court in London from 1674 to 1913, has a dedicated page, 'Irish London', at **www.oldbaileyonline.org/static/Irish.jsp**. Additional records will be held in local county record offices and archives across Britain.

Transportation

Various crimes in Ireland attracted a sentence of transportation to Australia, sometimes for a set period of years, and in others permanently. The NAI has some records documenting such cases, although all transportation registers pre-dating 1836 were destroyed in the Four Courts fire in 1922. The surviving materials include:

- Transportation Registers, 1836–1857;
- Prisoners' Petitions and Cases, 1788–1836;
- State Prisoners' Petitions, 1798–1799;
- Convict Reference Files, 1836–1856: 1865–1868;
- Free Settlers' Papers, 1828–1852; (f) Male Convict Register, 1842–1847;
- Register of Convicts on Convict Ships, 1851–1853.

CASE STUDY: A search of the NAI's Ireland-Australia transportation database for potential convicts from the County Tipperary town of Carrick-on-Suir shows the conviction of two brothers, Michael and John Greene. Both were sentenced in 1825 to seven years' transportation for the crime of manslaughter, with their entries recording that they had been imprisoned in Clonmel, and that both had previously resided in Carrick-on-Suir with their mother and six sisters. The document dated 13 May 1825 refers to a petition seeking their release (catalogued as PPC 2167).

The British Newspaper Archive offers a possible insight into the nature of their crime, with an article that only refers to a John Green, without his brother Michael. The *Dublin Evening Mail* of Monday, 25 October 1824 reported that:

Carrick-on-Suir, Co. Tipperary.

> A man named James English, of Carrick-on-Suir, has been stabbed so violently in the side and neck by a monster of the name of John Green, that he is not expected to recover. He has been arrested by the police.

The petition for the boys' release was clearly unsuccessful, as the 'New South Wales, Australia, Convict Indents, 1788–1842' on Ancestry informs us that both boys had sailed to Sydney Cove on board the *Sir Godfrey Webster*, arriving there on 3 January 1826. John was stated to be aged 36, Roman Catholic, and convicted at Clonmel, with a description noting that he had a ruddy complexion, brown hair and light grey eyes, and a tattoo on his right arm. His conduct was noted as 'well', and the document notes that he had never received any education. His brother Michael was aged just 23, Roman Catholic, had a dark sallow complexion, with light brown hair and light hazel eyes, and a slight scar on his left eyebrow. His conduct was also noted as being well, and unlike his brother, he could read. However, a note beneath his entry states that in 1828 his brother reported to the authorities in Sydney that Michael had died. The word 'brothers' was also noted, written vertically across both of their entries. A separate document found on Ancestry.com also notes that their crime was manslaughter, and gives their heights, with both brothers stated to be 6ft tall.

John was later noted in the 'New South Wales, Australia, Certificates of Freedom, 1810–1814, 1827–1867' database as having been granted a certificate of freedom on 23 March 1832, having completed his seven-year sentence. He remained in Australia, and is later found in the 'New South Wales, Australia, Gaol Description and Entrance Books, 1818–1930' database as having been committed to Sydney Gaol on several occasions between 1835 and 1841.

A dedicated NAI guide is available at **www.nationalarchives.ie/article/penal-transportation-records-ireland-australia-1788–1868/**, which includes access to the NAI's Ireland-Australia transportation database. A further guide on convict transportation from the UK National Archives is available at **www.nationalarchives.gov.uk/help-with-your-research/research-guides/criminal-transportation/**.

Down County Museum today is based at Downpatrick Gaol, an old convict gaol which held convicts to be transported to New South Wales from 1796 to 1830. A database held at the museum documents over 400 convicts to have been transported, about 1 per cent of estimated 45,000 to 55,000 prisoners transported. For further details see **www.visitmournemountains.co.uk/museums/down-county-museum/history-of-the-site/gaol-convicts-database** and **www.visitmournemountains.co.uk/museums/down-county-museum/history-of-the-site/transportation**.

In addition to these there are of course a substantial number of records in Australia itself that have survived. The Convicts to Australia guide at **http://perthdps.com/convicts/** can help, while available records online include many substantial databases for New South Wales and Australian convicts detailed at **www.ancestry.co.uk/search/categories/auconvicts/**. This includes one specific database concerning Irish dependents, the 'New South Wales, Australia, Wives & Children of Irish Convicts, 1825–1840' collection. Additional convict related records are available online through Findmypast and TheGenealogist.

Executions

Under the influence of the Brehon laws (p.75), capital punishment was rare, with murderers usually fined by way of punishment. However, if a fine was not paid, the guilty party could be executed. This situation slowly changed over the following centuries as the remit of English law extended across the island, imposed as the dominant legal infrastructure from the early seventeenth century.

During the period of the discriminatory Penal Laws, several acts were deemed to be capital crimes attracting a death sentence, although most were repealed by the end of the eighteenth century. However, in the eighteenth and nineteenth centuries various other crimes attracted the death penalty as part of Britain's 'Bloody Code', based on a series of Acts of Parliament passed at Westminster designed to protect the propertied classes. These included a range of felonies, from arson and murder to stealing from rabbit warrens and from shipwrecks.

Following the Judgment of Death Act of 1823, judges could pass less severe sentences than death for many of the crimes covered by the Code (this act was eventually repealed in Northern Ireland in 1980, and in the Republic in 1983). In 1828 the Criminal Law (Ireland) Act stated that crimes could be treated as capital crimes only if they were explicitly stated to be of that nature by Parliament after the passing of the act; this had the effect of substituting transportation or imprisonment for many previous crimes previously considered to be punishable by execution. The Offences Against the Person Act 1861 later decreed that there were just three capital offences, being murder, treason, and piracy with

> **CASE STUDY:** While the Crown insisted on the death penalty for many capital offences, there was by no means universal support for its stance by those required to stand as jurors, who were sometimes pressured into returning a guilty verdict against their better judgement.
>
> The Dublin based *Saunders's News-Letter* of Wednesday, 6 March 1799 reported that on the previous Friday, 1 March, four men by the name of John Quinn, Thomas Cavan, James Finsmere and Michael Sex, were prosecuted at the Dublin Commission Court (p.79) for burglary and robbery at the house of a Mr Wright Pike, resident at Milltown Road. The jury retired at 3.00 p.m. to deliberate on their fate, but when they returned at 4.00 p.m. they informed the judges that all but one of the jurors believed them to be guilty, with the dissenting juror refusing to state why he disagreed. The jury was instructed to retire once again until they could come up with a verdict.
>
> Deliberation on the case continued throughout the evening and the rest of the night, and when the judges returned the following morning, the jury was brought back before them at 10 a.m. Far from having an agreed verdict, however, the foreman informed the judge that they still had not come to a unanimous decision. The incensed judge ordered them to once again retire, and told them that they must continue to deliberate into Sunday should they have to. Having left to discuss the case further, the jurors returned to the courtroom within an hour to finally declare their unanimous verdict of guilty.
>
> It was at this point that the dissenting juror, a schoolmaster by the name of Forbes, from Glassmanogue, revealed that his resistance to the guilty verdict had been because 'he did not like a man should be hanged for any crime but murder'. The four men were sentenced to be executed on the following Saturday.

violence – the act also included what would today be considered to be anti-terrorist clauses, in this case with regards to the use of gunpowder to cause injury, reflecting the Fenian movement's campaign of the time.

During the period from 1916 to 1923, there were various executions, with the British executing many of the leaders and participants of the Easter Rising and War of Independence. With the creation of the Republican *Dáil* courts (p.82) during the War of Independence, a parallel process of corporal punishment continued through the courts martial processes of the IRA. Following the creation of the Free State in 1922, capital punishment was retained, with additional powers granted to the

CASE STUDY: Joseph Kelly's execution was carried out at 8.30 a.m. on 11 August 1863 in front of Wexford Jail, before a crowd of 500 people, the first such act to be performed in the county in 28 years. Kelly had murdered a cousin's husband, schoolmaster Michael Fitzhenry of Rathgarogue.

On the night before his death Kelly penned a confession, as recorded in the *Dublin Weekly Nation* of Saturday, 15 August 1863 (p.5):

> As a caution to those who are fond of drinking heavily, I think it right to make this declaration known to the public. On 17 May last, when I left New Ross, in the company of poor Michael Fitzhenry, I had not, according to the best of my belief, the intention of killing him, but I intended to give a great beating to him, because he would not give a suit of clothes to my dear father, according to contract, and also for some other trifling causes. After I had given him a few blows I left him lying alive on the road. I went off on my way home about a quarter of a mile, and then became afraid that that when he would recover he would prosecute me, and I would be punished severely. In order to prevent such punishment, and having drunk heavily, though I was not drunk, and being tempted by the Devil, I returned to the place where Fitzhenry was lying and committed the dreadful crime for which I am now justly about to suffer death. I am heartily sorry for this horrible crime, and all the scandal I have given. I die in peace and charity with all men. I humbly ask for the prayers of the faithful for the happy repose of my soul. I beg of the Mother of my God, the Blessed Virgin Mary, and St Joseph, to intercede for me now and at the moment of my death. May Christ Jesus, who said to the penitent thief 'This day shalt thou be with me in Paradise' – may the merits of His precious blood obtain mercy for me, a most miserable sinner.
>
> Joseph Kelly (his mark)
> Witnesses George Sutton, Clerk, Edward Cox, Turnkey.
> Wexford Jail, 10 August, 1863.

On the day itself, Kelly was resigned to his fate, but when on the scaffold, he asked if he could step forward to ask the crowd to pray

> for him. The Reverend Mr Roche, who had accompanied him, did so on his behalf, with the article noting that
>
>> the reverend gentlemen stepped out and called to the crowd to kneel and pray for the soul of the man who was about to die. The entire of the spectators were at once on their knees, and remained so until all was over.
>
> Shortly after 8.30 a.m., the time had come for Kelly's execution.
>
>> The signal having been given, the bolt of the trap was withdrawn, and he fell, a cry of mingled fright and horror at the same time rising from the still kneeling crowd outside. One of the policemen on duty fainted off the instant he saw the body fall. Death was evidently instantaneous, for not a single movement was observable in the body after it fell. After having hung for three quarters of an hour it was let down, placed in a coffin, and buried at the back of the jail.
>
> Joseph Kelly's execution was the last to be carried out before the general public, five years before the law was changed to make such events private behind prison walls.

new National Army (which emerged from the pro-Treaty wing of the IRA) to carry out executions by firing squad for those convicted through special courts martial.

Following Partition, the Free State continued to employ executions for capital offences based on the legal mechanisms previously established by the British, with death sentences carried out either by firing squad or by the hangman. The South's Treason Act of 1939 imposed the death penalty for treason, which was not removed from statute until 1990. The majority of hangings in the Free State and later the Republic were carried out by notorious British hangman Thomas Pierrepoint at Mountjoy Prison in Dublin, with the last three hangings carried out by his nephew Albert.

Michael Manning was the last person to be hanged in the Republic, for having raped and murdered 65-year-old nurse Catherine Cooper on 15 November 1953 in Limerick, with his execution taking place at Dublin's Mountjoy Prison on 20 April 1954. Manning was the thirty-fifth person to be executed in the South following Partition, being preceded

Memorial to four IRA volunteers executed by the Free State Army in Kilmainham Gaol in 1922.

by William Downes, Thomas Delaney, Thomas McDonagh, Peter Hynes (1923), Jeremiah Gaffney, Felix McMullen (1924), Cornelius O'Leary, Annie Walsh, Michael Talbot (1925), James Myles, James McHugh, Henry McCabe (1926), William O'Neill (1927), Gerard Toal (1928), John Cox (1929), David O'Shea (1931), Patrick McDermott (1932), John Fleming (1934), John Hornick (1937), Dermot Smith (1939), Patrick McGrath, Thomas Harte (1940), Daniel Doherty, Henry Gleeson, Richard Goss, Patrick Kelly (1941), George Plant, Maurice O'Neill (1942), Bernard Kirwan, William O'Shea (1943), Charles Kerins (1944), James Lehman (1945), Joseph McManus (1947), and William Gambon (1948). All but two were executed at Mountjoy Prison, mostly by hanging (with three by firing squad), while Richard Goss and George Plant were shot dead by firing squad at Portlaoise Prison.

A decade after Manning's death, capital punishment in the South was largely abolished from 1964, although it remained a possibility for those convicted of the murders of Gardai, prison officers and diplomats. It was eventually removed from the country's statutes entirely in 1990, with the Irish Constitution amended in 2001 to remove all references to it. Relevant court papers are held at the National Archives of Ireland, but cannot be searched for via the online catalogue; for further details consult **www.nationalarchives.ie/legal-records/researching-legal-records/**.

The last person executed in Northern Ireland was 26-year-old Robert McGladdery, who was hanged at Crumlin Road Gaol at 8 a.m. on Wednesday, 20 December 1961, for the murder of 19-year-old Pearl Gamble near Newry in February of that year. Part of McGladdery's trial transcript and papers are open to view at PRONI, catalogued under HA/20/A/1/68A and HA/31/2/87/1A, although additional papers under HA/20/A/1/68 and HA/31/2/87/1 are closed to public access until 2061. McGladdery was the tenth individual to have been executed at the gaol since Partition, following the executions of Simon McGeown (1922), Michael Pratley (1924), William Smiley (1928), Samuel Cushnahan (1930), Thomas Dornan (1931), Eddie Cullens (1932), Harold Courtney (1933), Thomas Williams (1942), and Samuel McLaughlin (1961). All were buried within the walls of the gaol, although the bodies of Thomas Williams and Michael Pratley have since been exhumed and reburied elsewhere.

Although capital punishment was suspended from 1965 in Britain, and abolished from 1969, it was not until the 1973 Northern Ireland (Emergency Provisions) Act that it was suspended in Northern Ireland, and not removed from statute until 1998, with treason remaining the only remaining crime that could attract such a sentence until that point.

The Capital Punishment UK platform at **www.capitalpunishmentuk.org/ir1835.html** details the names of 237 people executed across Ireland between 1835 and 1899, as well as the names of their victims. The site also notes details of all twentieth century executions in the North convicted in the criminal courts at **www.capitalpunishmentuk.org/nirish.html**, and similarly for the South at **www.capitalpunishmentuk.org/ireland.html**.

Chapter 4

POVERTY AND HEALTH

Poverty was a huge factor that could lead to the decline of health and future prospects, and all of us will have ancestors somewhere along the line who suffered financial hardship. To try to deal with this, the state's implementation of the Poor Relief (Ireland) Act 1838 led to many massive changes in how the needs of the destitute poor and the most vulnerable were addressed, albeit initially with 'tough love' measures.

As is true for us, our ancestors will also have suffered from various maladies in the past, from the common cold to more life-threatening illnesses. For many of our forebears folk medicines and superstition were often the only defences against the potential troubles that could befall them. Over time science increasingly began to assert itself to provide more effective remedies, while the state itself began to implement solutions to try to prevent health issues emerging in the first place.

A cause of death on a certificate can often provide us with a glimpse into the ultimate challenges faced and lost by our ancestors, albeit with language that has constantly changed over the years. Tuberculosis, for example, a major problem in the nineteenth and early twentieth century, was previously known by many names, including 'phthisis pulmonalis', 'consumption', and 'decline', while the recording of 'syncope', as in 'cardiac syncope', means that the patient suddenly lost consciousness before death. Terminal illnesses were not the only problems that affected our forebears however, and various hospitals were established to help those at all stages of life, with the local workhouse infirmary often acting as a major treatment centre for many.

Epidemics were also prevalent in the past. While today the elderly and most vulnerable in our population can receive a flu jab each winter, a hundred years ago influenza was a huge killer, with some 21,000 people dying between the spring of 1918 and spring 1919 during the first wave of the 'Spanish Flu' pandemic – a huge number when compared to the estimated 30,000 Irishmen who died fighting in the First World War within the British Army's Irish regiments.

In this chapter I will examine how governments addressed the challenges of poverty and health within the population, describing the institutions established, and some of the records generated that might assist for research.

The Poor Law

One of the first workhouses erected in Ireland was in 1703 in Dublin, which held up to 160 men and women, and which from 1730 also took in foundlings (p.43). In 1752 the Belfast Charitable Society established itself at Clifton House, and after a significant fundraising endeavour opened a poor house in 1774 to help with the distress of the town's most destitute inhabitants. The Society's Heritage Centre today offers access to records for researchers, including applications forms for those seeking relief, and admissions books detailing inhabitants from 1805 to 1882, which may name their next of kin, their religious denomination, their residential addresses, and when and how they were eventually discharged (see **https://cliftonbelfast.com/collections/**). An additional workhouse was

Clifton House was established as a poor house in Belfast in 1752 by the Belfast Charitable Society.

also erected in Cork from 1747, and a House of Industry in Limerick from 1774. For more on these institutions visit Peter Higginbotham's excellent Workhouses website at **www.workhouses.org.uk/Ireland**.

Following the Poor Law (Amendment) Act of 1834 in England and Wales, Ireland would receive its own 'Act for the more effectual Relief of the Destitute Poor in Ireland' on 31 July 1838, aka the 'Poor Relief (Ireland) Act 1838' (**www.irishstatutebook.ie/eli/1838/act/56/enacted/en/print.html**), passed as part of a response to deter Irish emigration to Britain. A new regime was implemented to raise taxation for the relief of the poor, which permitted the country to be carved up into a series of 137 'poor law unions', with borders drawn up by the Poor Law Boundary Commission. These were based on previous electoral divisions that had been created from groupings of townlands across the country, and not on parishes. A workhouse was established in each union, and by 1850 the set-up was extended further to 163 poor law unions.

Each poor law union had a board of guardians to oversee the provision of poor relief, whose members were elected locally with the purpose of overseeing its daily administration. The 1838 Act specifically precluded ministers or priests from any religious denomination to become members, although each workhouse was to cater for religious services.

Section 41 of the act outlined the priorities of relief to be implemented:

> When the commissioners shall have declared any workhouse of any union to be fit for the reception of destitute poor, and not before, it shall be lawful for the guardians, at their discretion, but subject in all cases to the orders of the commissioners, to take order for relieving and setting to work therein, in the first place, such destitute poor persons as by reason of old age, infirmity, or defect may be unable to support themselves, and destitute children, and, in the next place, such other persons as the said guardians shall deem to be destitute poor, and unable to support themselves by their own industry or by other lawful means.

Sections 53–54 of the act outlined where the initial responsibility lay within a household for the support of children:

> 53. For the purposes of this Act every husband shall be liable to maintain his wife, and every child under the age of fifteen, whether legitimate or illegitimate, which she may have had at the time of her marriage with such husband; and every father shall be liable to maintain his child, and every widow to maintain her child, and the

mother of every bastard child to maintain such bastard child, until every such child respectively shall attain the age of fifteen years: Provided always, and be it declared, that nothing herein contained shall be taken to remove or lessen the obligations to which any husband or parent is by law liable in regard to the maintenance of his wife or children, legitimate or illegitimate respectively, independently of this Act.

54. All relief given under this Act to a wife or child shall be considered as given to the person declared by this Act to be liable to maintain such wife or child.

Similar responsibilities for children were also stipulated with regards to supporting their elderly parents:

57. Where any poor person shall, through old age, infirmity, or defect, be unable to support himself, every child of such poor, person shall be liable, according to his ability, to support or contribute to support such poor person; and in case relief shall be given under this Act to any poor person whose child shall be liable to support him or contribute to his support, it shall be lawful for any two justices of the peace of the jurisdiction within which such child may dwell, on the application of the guardians of the union in which such relief shall have been given, by their order to direct what sum, not exceeding the cost price of such relief, shall be paid by such child to such guardians in respect of the relief which shall have been so given.

Financial relief could be made outright to a claimant, or determined to be a loan. For those in receipt of a pension or other income from the armed forces, such as Chelsea and Greenwich Pensioners, the guardians could redirect payments from Her Majesty's paymaster general to repay any money paid out by them.

The initial priority was to provide relief to the destitute poor only within a workhouse. Conditions were harsh, with children separated from their parents, and with all made to work, in a system that was deliberately made to be uncomfortable to encourage inmates to leave and seek employment. However, the advent of the Famine in the mid-1840s completely overwhelmed the workhouses, with the minute books of the guardians providing glimpses into the inadequate provision. For

CASE STUDY: Poor relief records can often help to build up a picture of families prior to the advent of civil registration, and beyond, particularly in areas where the relevant parish registers are not available.

For example, the admission records for the poor law union of Larne, Co. Antrim provide many entries for a Margaret Gordon, also known as Madge, who was born in the parish of Islandmagee in about 1839, and who was an adherent to the Church of Ireland, the records for which in Islandmagee have sadly not survived for this period. On 23 August 1859 Madge first entered the workhouse due to ill health, with the record noting her to be a single servant. She remained in Larne until 9 February 1860. Just over a year later, on 2 April 1861, she returned to the workhouse, this time because she was pregnant, and remained there until 28 August; it is likely that she gave birth in the workhouse, but no child is shown as having been with her upon her departure. Later in the same year it appears that she may have returned yet again, albeit erroneously noted as 24 years of age. On this occasion she was noted as a servant, and of good health, and remained in the institution until 1 March 1862.

For a couple of years Madge remained outside of the workhouse, but on 13 December 1864 she returned for just under a month, due to ill health, being eventually discharged on 8 January 1865. In this case the entry also noted her townland of residence in Islandmagee, it being Ballycronan.

Almost three years later she returned yet again, on 14 October 1868, now aged 30, and still a single servant. Madge was once again pregnant, with the register also noting that she was 'clean and well clad'. (Poor Relief. Indoor Register, Larne Workhouse. 14 October 1868. GORDON, Madge. BG/17/G/3. PRONI, Belfast.) The civil registration birth register informs us that she gave birth on 13 December 1868 to a son that she named James, who was added on the same day to the admission register. His entry notes his arrival as a 'bastard', that he was of the Church of Ireland ('established church'), and clean and well clad. Both James and his mother left the institution on 17 February 1869.

Records from the same union also provide a detailed picture for a relative of Madge's from Islandmagee, 56-year-old Mary Gordon, who was noted as having been admitted to the workhouse on 15 February 1863. In her admission entry Mary was described as a widow and a labourer from Brown's Bay in the parish of Islandmagee, a member of the 'established church', in 'bad health', and with her appearance described as 'middling'. On the same day, as noted in the very next entry, her son Henry Gordon, aged just 11, was also admitted, and noted as being in good health, and also of a 'middling' appearance. (Poor Relief. Indoor Register, Larne Workhouse. 15 February 1863. GORDON, Mary and Henry. BG/17/G/3. PRONI, Belfast.)

Tragically, their story in the workhouse was not to end well, with Mary dying there on 24 March 1863 – the only record of her death found to date, with the civil registration of deaths not commencing until the following year. Although in good health upon his arrival, young Henry also tragically died just over three months later in the same building, on 2 July 1863.

The former Larne Workhouse building today forms part of the Moyle Hospital, where the author was born in 1970.

example, in Irvinestown union (known as Lowtherstown at the time), a guardian called Henry D'Arcy witnessed the following:

> I happened to go to the Dormitories when the Paupers were going to bed, and anything more disgusting than the scene I witnessed could not be imagined, buckets are left in the middle of the floor, some of them leaking, to these the Paupers have recourse in all their wants, and the effluvia arising from it is insufferable. I am informed they do not go further than their bedside.

(Source: Irvinestown Board of Guardians minutes book, Dec 1848– Dec 1849, PRONI BG/15/A/4)

CASE STUDY: A typical example of the workhouse admissions' registers records concerns an application for a sister of one of my three times great-grandmothers.

Mary Jane Gibson was noted as having been admitted to the urban based Belfast Workhouse on 7 February 1891. The following were the questions asked of her, and the responses:

No.	1389
Name and surname of pauper	Gibson, Mary J
Sex	F
Age	33
If adult, whether single, married, widower or widow; if child whether orphaned, deserted or Bastard	Married
Employment or Calling	Mill
Religious denomination	Presby[terian]
If disabled, the description of disability	weak mind
Name of wife or husband	5 Cargill Street [sic]
No. of children	
Observation on condition of Pauper when admitted	
Electoral division and townland in which resident	Belfast
Date when admitted or when Born in Workhouse	7th Feb [18]91
Date when Died, or left the Workhouse	29th Feb [18]91

(Poor Relief, Ireland. Indoor Register, Belfast Workhouse. 7 February 1891. GIBSON, Mary J. BG/7/G/14, p.35 PRONI, Belfast)

In her civil death record, Mary's condition was described alternatively as 'dementia', rather than of 'weak mind'.

So overpopulated were the workhouses at this time that Earl Grey implemented a scheme to transport children to Australia, where they would be made to work as domestic labourers (p.51).

With changing attitudes towards the end of the century, outdoor relief became a more widespread alternative to workhouse admission.

The workhouse system was abandoned in the Free State following Partition. Many poor law records in the South were unfortunately destroyed during the War of Independence and the Civil War, although the minute books from some areas have survived. The NAI has a guide to using poor law records at **www.nationalarchives.ie/article/guide-archives-poor-law/**, although the archive's own holdings largely comprises those for the greater Dublin area and unions in counties Cavan and Sligo.

Some surviving records have been placed online. Poor law union minute books from Co. Clare can be found at **www.digitalbookindex.org/_search/search010hstirelandworkhousea.asp**, for example, while a substantial collection of workhouse admission and discharge registers for Dublin from 1840 to 1919 are available on Findmypast, alongside the city's board of guardians minute books. Some further limited offerings are also available on the site for workhouse records from unions in Clare, Waterford and Sligo. For further online offerings, or for records held locally, check the relevant county archive website for the area of interest.

The workhouse system continued in Northern Ireland until 1948, with records from the North's twenty-seven poor law unions held at PRONI in Belfast, catalogued under BG, with a guide available at **www.nidirect.gov.uk/publications/family-tree-poor-law-records**. The archive's online catalogue can be used to search an index to Belfast's admission registers from 1892 to 1921, with accession codes ranging from BG/7/GK/1 (July 1892 – October 1892) to BG/7/GK/107 (May 1921 – September 1921). A

> **TIP:** In addition to county archives, it is always worth checking out local museums and heritage centres for local resources. Many years ago I happened to visit Carrick-on-Suir Heritage Centre in County Tipperary and was surprised to discover a series of pawn shop books from 1864 to 1868 for the town in a locked glass cabinet, listing thousands of occurrences of the town's poorest folk seeking a few pennies here and there for their most prized possessions. I was given permission to examine them and after many hours of examination I found several new family members not heard of before, and much about those already discovered; for example, my wife's great-grandmother Johanna Donovan was noted as having pawned a pair of boots for four shillings and seven pence on Monday, 2 October 1865, aged just 17 at the time, with her address correctly noted as Oven Lane within Carrick-on-Suir.

full break down of coverage by period and reference is available in my book *Tracing Your Belfast Ancestors*.

For earlier periods, Findmypast also hosts records of loans given to the 'industrious poor' in the west of the country within its 'Ireland, Poverty Relief Loans 1821–1874' collection. Sourced from the National Archives in England (catalogued under T91), the documents concern the Irish Reproductive Loan Fund, which was established in 1822 as a credit scheme to help the industrious poor. The collection includes loan ledgers, security note books, account books, minute books, defaulters books and more. There are some 700,000 applications included, with most applications from the years 1824–1846.

Deportation of Irish Paupers From Britain

As part of the United Kingdom, many Irish people who settled in Britain tried to claim poor relief there as they would have done back home. If it was determined that they had no legal right of 'settlement' they could be deported from the nearest port back to their home parishes in Ireland, even if they had been in Britain for decades. The practice increased dramatically following the implementation of the English and Welsh Poor Law (Amendment) Act of 1834, four years before Ireland's own poor relief reforms were introduced.

The now defunct Moving Here website cites a good example of the types of records you might find in British county record offices and local archives at **https://web.archive.org/web/20130411042902/http://movinghere.org.uk/galleries/histories/irish/settling/removal_1.htm**. Among the records illustrated is a digitised copy of one of sixty-five volumes from 1801 to 1835 recording the names of poor people who were deported from Liverpool to Ireland, in this case from the year 1834, as sourced from Lancashire Record Office. The site also gives examples of other useful records, including the original examination papers relating to an individual's case, as well as material relating to the removal as held in the relevant quarter sessions' papers for the area in question.

The ProQuest UK Parliamentary Papers website, accessed through subscribing libraries and universities at **https://parlipapers.proquest.com/parlipapers**, contains further lengthy lists naming people so removed; locate such entries through its catalogue using search terms such as 'poor removal' and a date range. The earlier nineteenth century records on the platform tend to concern various bills and legislation about the poor laws themselves. Records listing removals in this period are usually more statistical in nature, with most not naming those who were removed, and instead providing the numbers of those ejected from

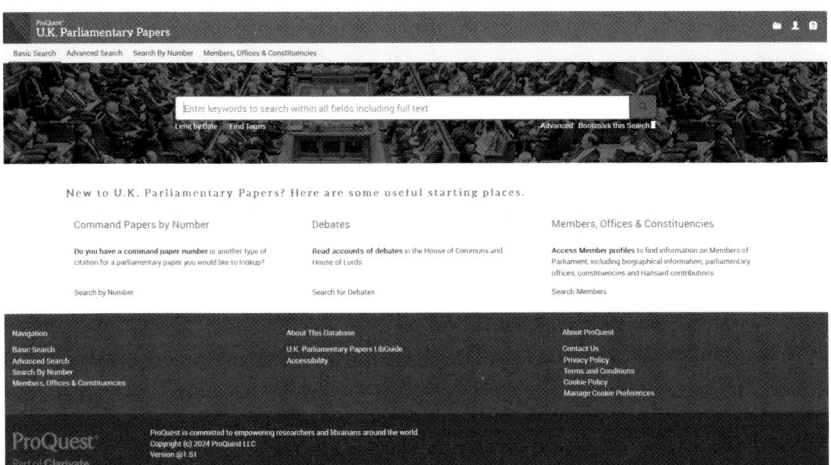

The ProQuest UK Parliamentary Papers website can help to locate information on Irish poor law removals from Britain.

each parish with any associated costs. It is not until later in the century when more genealogically useful material begins to appear on the site.

The first detailed list of paupers on the site is that published in 1863 detailing all the destitute poor removed from England and Scotland and sent back to Ireland between 1 December 1860 and 1 December

> **CASE STUDY:** Documentation on the UK Parliamentary Papers website concerning poor law removals from Britain can be immensely detailed. An example from July 1867 notes the case of 27-year-old Mary Horrigan, wife of a marine from the north of Ireland called Michael Horrigan, who had left Skibbereen, County Cork, at the age of 1.
>
> Seven months after her husband went to China to serve, Mary applied for poor relief from Greenwich Union, but was ordered to leave Woolwich for Skibbereen, even though her four children had been born in England. Upon reaching Skibbereen, she was duly sent back to London by the union there. Correspondence over her circumstances was included in a poor removal return to the House of Commons dated 24 May 1870.
>
> In another example, from 1875, a Margaret Gillespie is noted by the authorities in Sunderland within a list of removals describing her deportation to Belfast. Although her age is not recorded, the record states that she had two children, 4-year-old Mary Ellen and 6-month-old Charles, and that she had resided in England for seventeen years, though with a 'considerable time spent in Scotland'. The reason for her removal is given as her 'inability to earn a livelihood'.

1862. Several similar reports then follow, with the latest equivalent list dating from 1878. The records are surprisingly detailed and list many individuals and their causes for removal, but are unfortunately not keyword searchable. This means that you will have to browse your way through them to the parish of interest. In most cases the counties and parishes are presented in alphabetical order, although the names of the individuals are not so arranged within each parish list.

Not every case in the records documents those who were forcibly removed, with some cases of voluntary resettlements also included.

> **TIP:** If you cannot gain access to the Parliamentary Papers website, some of the records are also freely available on Raymond's County Down website at **www.raymondscountydownwebsite.com**. These include returns from Scotland to Ireland in 1867, 1869 and 1875–8, and from England and Wales to Ireland in 1867, 1869, as well as from January 1875.

Hospitals and Public Health

Day to day life in Ireland's more urbanised communities presented many challenges to the public health of the residents. The Town Book of the Corporation of Belfast, for example, notes details of a complaint dealt with by the Corporation on 7 January 1663 concerning the nuisance caused by the work of butchers within the town, and the body's response:

> That whereas dayly complaintes are made by severall Inhabitants of the said Borrough that great annoyance is comitted by the Butchers of this Towne by killing and slaughtering of Catle they suffer the Blood and Garbage of their slaughter houses, some to lye in ye streets & other parte to run into several channells and ditches of this Towne to corruption and putrefaccon of the River and anoyance of their neighbours by reason of the stinke and evill and infectious smell (that if not timely prevented) will by all likelyhood bringe some Ruinous and pestellentiall desease among ye Inhabitants, which for the future that care may be taken and such enormityes cured, It is ordered and by and with the consent afforesd it is hereby enacted that if any Butcher or Butchers or any other person whatsoever shall from and after the date hereof slaughter or kill or cause to slaughtered or killed any catle of what kinde soever within this Towne of Belfast without they or any of them soe doing shall carry cause to be carryed the same day all ye

Blood and Garbage of such beasts or catle soe killed or slaughtered twenty yards beyon ye full sea marke every such Butcher or other person offending herein shall for every offence pay twenty shillings sterling to be levied immediately by distresse or otherwise as is accustomed &c.

As such urban settlements grew, diseases such as smallpox, scarlatina, typhus, whooping-cough and cholera (known contemporaneously as the 'zymotic diseases') could appear on a localised basis, or nationwide. Although for the island as a whole the mortality rates were lower than in Britain, the rates within the largest cities matched many of those in Scotland and England.

Charitable dispensaries, funded by subscriptions from the local gentry, did their best to treat those afflicted, and to prevent the spread of disease into epidemic proportions. From 1774 the Belfast Charitable Society, for example, provided medical relief at the poor house at Clifton Street (p.113), annually offering hundreds of its citizens treatment. However, such relief was not extended to those who had lost their employment due to ill health, or to those who did not have the right of settlement. To address this deficiency, a general dispensary was created in the city in 1792, with funds raised by subscription, with its committee working in partnership with the Charitable Society.

These institutions worked alongside county infirmaries, founded by the Irish Parliament in 1765, and fever hospitals, to hold the line against public health threats. However, provision was patchy across the island beyond the major urban settlements; for example, in County Mayo in 1836 there was a county infirmary and just a single medical dispensary, for a population of 200,000, mainly from the labouring class.

In 1817, a major epidemic of typhus spread across the island, the population having already to an extent been weakened by food shortages caused by a bad harvest in the previous year, as well as a wet summer that had made it impossible to dry enough peat for winter fuel in the thousands of cottages across the land. The British government converted Dublin's barracks and prisons into temporary infirmaries, to assist the city's overwhelmed hospitals. Between September 1817 and June 1819, 40,594 patients were admitted, of whom 1,919 died of the fever, with thousands more dying across the entire island; one contemporary estimate noted the death toll to be as high as 44,600, out of 737,000 cases, five times the official figures of 6,100 deaths from 149,000 cases, as recorded by the nation's hospitals.

TIP: The reports of sanitary committees and medical officers of health reports can be particularly informative reading, with reports for many areas of the country such as Belfast, Dublin, Cork, Donegal, Down, Kilkenny, Louth and Lurgan via the Wellcome Library catalogue at **https://wellcomecollection.org**.

If we look at the report to the Sanitary Committee of Dublin Corporation drawn up in 1865, for example, the Medical Officer of Health for Dublin, E.D. Mapother, starts by providing an overview of the mortality picture for the city, noting that in 1865 there were 6,959 deaths, a rate of 28 per 1,000, which compared favourably to cities in England and Scotland, such as London and its suburbs (1 in 38), central London (1 in 37) and Glasgow (1 in 30). In greater detail, however, he then pointed out the varying rates across Dublin's seven districts, which were named after the streets where the dispensary station was based:

North side:
Summer Hill   1 in 55
Coleraine Street   1 in 50
Blackhall Street   1 in 23

South side:
Meath Street   1 in 22
High Street   1 in 49
Peter Street   1 in 46
Grand Canal Street 1 in 57

Of the 1,483 'zymotic' deaths (p.113), 492 were down to fever, with the highest number of cases in the following streets:

North side:
Church Street, Beresford Street, Greek Street, North King Street, Barrack Street, Lower Mecklenburgh Street, and Cole's Lane.

South side:
Coombe, Skinner's Alley, Meath Street, Patrick Street, West Essex Street, Townsend Street, Poolbeg Street, and Wood Quay.

There were also 70 deaths to smallpox, 43 to scarlatina, 157 to measles, 290 to dysentery and cholera, 969 deaths to consumption (tuberculosis), and 511 infant deaths to convulsions. For the latter, the officer noted that it was to be hoped that new bylaws to be introduced compelling tenement dwellings to have glazed moveable windows, and proper sewerage systems, would have a dramatic impact by providing better access to fresh air and sunlight.

(Mapother, E.D. (1865) *Report of the Health of Dublin for the Year 1865*. Dublin, Edward Dillon. **https://wellcomecollection.org/works/zqazmuqs/items**: accessed 30 October 2024)

Another major pestilence to scourge the nation was the Asiatic cholera from April 1832, believed to have been brought over from Liverpool in England to the ports of Belfast and Dublin. Cholera had a far higher mortality rate than typhus for those who contracted it – in Sligo alone, out of the estimated 1,500 people who contracted the disease, 641 died – but the epidemic was shorter, having run its course by October of that year.

Shortly after the cholera wave had ended, a series of reforms began to improve the way that the state tackled such epidemiological outbreaks, starting with the 1838 Poor Law Ireland Act, and the establishment of workhouses in each poor law union, to which an infirmary was attached. During the Famine, disease continued to spread, caused by dysentery and a more virulent cholera epidemic in 1849, which hit those seeking relief within the many packed workhouses.

As a consequence, in 1851 the Medical Charities Act provided medical dispensaries in each of the country's poor law unions, each with a medical officer paid for by the poor rate, whose job it was to provide medical care and medicines to the sick poor. (There had previously been just a handful of such dispensaries, as established under a former grand jury based network.) For the first time the poorest across society could now seek the services of a doctor at home, with free medical care. While workhouse hospitals had catered for the destitute sick from inception, a further change occurred with the Poor Law (Amendment) Act 1862, which now allowed the non-destitute sick to be treated at workhouse hospitals, further expanding the options for medical treatment within communities.

Public health reforms continued with the Towns Improvement Act of 1854, which empowered local authorities to deal with sanitation issues and to reform building regulations. By far the biggest reform, however, was in 1878 with the passage of the first Public Health Act (**www.irishstatutebook.ie/eli/1878/act/52/enacted/en/print.html**), which carved the whole country up into a series of urban and rural sanitary districts, working to the relevant local government board (the successor to the poor law commissioners). The sanitary authorities now had the power to compel the construction of better sewage and clean water facilities, as well as to regulate various polluting industries, such as slaughter houses; in subsequent years they gained additional powers, such as to regulate milk production, with poor milk being one cause for infant mortality.

While the state health care infrastructure was developing, private facilities also continued. During the First World War, for example, the Ulster Volunteer Force, which emerged as part of the anti-Home Rule movement (p.136), contributed thousands of recruits to the British Army. To assist with their care, a hospital was established at Craigavon House,

---

CASE STUDY: During the Spanish flu outbreak, the death register for Carrick-on-Suir in County Tipperary noted the passing of two relatives of my wife, being two sisters who passed away on the same weekend within the same house, both having contracted influenza in their twenties.

The first to pass away on 25 March 1922 was 25-year-old housekeeper Mary Anne Colleton, who had suffered from the illness for three weeks. Her 29-year-old sister Margaret, a creamery worker in the town, died a day later on the 26th, she too having suffered from flu for three weeks, although her recorded cause of death also noted cardiac failure. Their brother Patrick registered both deaths.

The tragic story made the local press in Co. Kilkenny:

FLU TRAGEDY

TWO SISTERS' DEATH IN CARRICK

Two sisters (Margaret and Mary Anne Colleton, of Greystone Street, Carrick-on-Suir), died from influenza – one on Saturday and the other on Sunday. The deceased were aged between twenty and thirty. The funeral of one took place on Monday and of the other on Tuesday, and both funerals were largely attended.

(*Kilkenny Moderator* (1922). Flu Tragedy. Saturday, 1 April. p.4. www.britishnewspaperarchive.co.uk: accessed 30 October 2024)

known as the 'UVF Hospital', to deal with soldiers suffering from shell-shock, with a separate care facility established at Belfast Corporation's Exhibition Hall. The hospital continued its work after both world wars, but with the outbreak of the Troubles in 1969 it renamed itself as the Somme Hospital, to distinguish itself from the newly emerged paramilitary group that had appropriated the name of the UVF; a history of the facility can be found at **https://bit.ly/SommeHospital**.

Despite the improving infrastructure in Ireland, there would be many more challenges to come in ensuing decades, including the scourge of tuberculosis from the late nineteenth century to the early twentieth century, and the 'Spanish flu' epidemic from spring 1918 to spring 1919. While the introduction of the civil registration of deaths in Ireland from January 1864 provided the establishment with a better means to work out mortality rates and to shape public policy, the records from this point also reveal many tragedies at a local level.

Following Partition, the workhouse system in the Free State was abolished, and county boards of health created in their wake, with many of the workhouse buildings closed and others repurposed as hospitals or county homes for the aged and infirm. In 1930 a lottery known as the Irish Hospitals Sweepstake led to a huge programme of investment in the state's medical infrastructure, with the first new hospital constructed in Mullingar in 1936, Westmeath County Hospital.

The National Archives of Ireland hosts the fascinating Survey of Hospital Archives in Ireland, funded by the Wellcome Trust, which sought to identify all hospital archives held locally in the Republic of Ireland through a survey carried out between May 2014 and December 2015. The report is available at **https://web.archive.org/web/20240917110108/https://www.nationalarchives.ie/wp-content/uploads/2019/03/PRF_106780_SURVEY_OF_HOSPITAL_BOOK_V7.pdf**, and includes a useful overview by archivist Brian Donnelly of the development of hospitals in Ireland, a handy glossary of terms related to the administration of the hospitals sector, and detailed reports from each county on holdings available locally. The National Archive itself holds many hospital records, with a useful guide listing holdings available at **www.nationalarchives.ie/article/guide-hospital-records/**.

For Northern Ireland, PRONI holds a substantial collection of records, which are closed for a hundred years after the date of the last register entry. There is no research guide for the records on its website, but they are well catalogued. The archive also hosts a digitised register for the Royal Victoria Hospital from 1914 to 1916 at **www.nidirect.gov.uk/articles/royal-victoria-hospital-register-1914–1916**, detailing the many war casualties it treated in this period, which can also be searched on Ancestry through its 'Belfast, Antrim, Ireland, Royal Victoria Hospital Register, 1914–1916' database. The register notes the names and ranks of patients, their regiments and service numbers, when admitted and discharged, and the cost for their treatment.

Asylums

Mental illness was something that was often hidden by families in the past, with afflicted relatives committed to asylums – and in many cases, left there for decades. There were various causes that could lead to mental illness, from depression to the effects of physical diseases, but for many in the public the presence of a relative in an asylum could lead to stigma. In some situations, the system was abused, with people committed to institutions simply to get them out of the way, for example to remove them from a future inheritance, or because of marital disharmony.

The state care for the mentally ill in Ireland can be traced back to the eighteenth century, when two acts of the Irish Parliament in 1772 and 1787 had tried to encourage grand juries to fund lunatic wards within county workhouses, which largely failed. It would not be until July 1817 that the British state authorised the creation of the first centralised asylum system in Ireland for what were termed the 'lunatic poor', decades before an equivalent system was introduced in Britain itself. By the start of the twentieth century there were more than 20,000 inmates in institutions across Ireland.

Following the Lunacy (Ireland) Act of 1821, a new Board of Commissioners in Lunacy was created to oversee a new system of district asylums, which were gradually implemented across the country throughout the nineteenth century. The newly built asylums were established in Armagh (1825), Limerick (1827), Belfast (1829), Londonderry and Carlow (1832), Maryborough and Ballinasloe (1833), Clonmel (1834), Waterford (1835), Killarney and Kilkenny (1852), Omagh (1853), Mullingar and Sligo (1855), Castlebar and Letterkenny (1866), Ennis and Enniscorthy (1868), Downpatrick and Monaghan (1869), Portrane (Co. Dublin, 1903), and Holywell (Co. Antrim, 1899).

No sooner were these erected than they were almost overcome by demand; for example, the asylum erected on Belfast's Grosvenor Road in 1829, initially designed to hold a hundred patients, had triple that number within a few short years. Following its closure in 1913, the building was converted to be used by the Royal Belfast Maternity Hospital from 1933, while the asylum's work continued at the new Purdysburn Villa Colony, which became a hospital in 1948, and later Knockbracken Mental Health Services.

When the poor law system was established from 1838, lunatic wards were created in the newly established workhouses, but these were managed separately to the district asylums, as were a series of licensed privately run institutions, such as Hampstead House and Highfield House in Dublin. In addition were a series of voluntary asylums, run on a not-for-profit charitable basis, and with religious connections, which included St Patrick's Hospital for Imbeciles in Kilmainham, established in 1757 thanks to money bequeathed for the purpose by Jonathan Swift, the author of *Gulliver's Travels* (which continues today as St Patrick's University Hospital). It would not be until 1842 that the government had a formal say in the licensing and running of private institutions, following the Private Asylums (Ireland) Act, although voluntary asylums, being charitable in nature, were exempted from being licensed. Following the passage of the Lunacy Act 1845, all Irish asylums would become subject to the oversight of lunacy inspectors based in Dublin Castle from 1846, staffed by medically qualified appointees.

The public asylum system in Ireland was overcrowded, often receiving patients from workhouses, and others who were not in fact mentally ill, but placed within them as a convenient solution by other members of the family unwilling to look after them. The system of private asylums was not much better at times, with the vested interest of their shareholders often trumping the need for proper fully funded medical care.

While the majority of those admitted did suffer from mental illness, the earliest inmates only had the treatment of a physician if they were suffering from a bodily disease that was known to induce insanity. The reports from asylums at the time can give an impression of the work carried out within them, including their success rates for curing inmates. The *Cork Constitution* from Saturday, 22 March 1828, for example, offers the second report of the Cork Lunatic Asylum, as presented to its Board of Governors. This noted that just over a year earlier there had been 257 inmates at the institution, which had increased within a year to 378. Of these, seventy-two were said to have been cured, thirteen relieved and discharged, while twenty-five had died, and five deemed to be 'improper'. On 1 March 1828, there were still 262 inmates within the institution.

CASE STUDY: In October 1842 a story gripped the nation for weeks concerning immorality stated to have occurred at Carlow Lunatic Asylum. It was alleged that a young female housemaid, 15-year-old Mary Keefe, had been raped three times by the asylum manager, Patrick McCaffrey, and had become pregnant as a consequence. An inquiry was duly established, led by Henry Martley QC and Dr Francis White, the inspector of prisons. On Saturday, 5 November 1842, the *English Chronicle and Whitehall Evening Press* reported the following from the proceedings:

> The charges against the manager are of a most serious nature, and refer to the forcible violation of a young girl, about 15 years of age, a servant to the gate-keeper; and we fear, from what we learn, that the conduct of the subordinate officers, and indeed of all the servants, is of such a nature as to warrant the most searching inquiry, which we are happy to hear is being made by the commissioners, whose judgment, ability and impartiality, our correspondent speaks most favourably. It is now manifest that the institution requires a thorough reformation, and we shall show the extent to which the reform should be carried, the moment we are at liberty to publish the evidence; but pending the inquiry we shall offer no observation tending to pre-judge the case, or that may be likely to affect the character of the individuals concerned. There are two of the keepers also charged, the one with tampering with the witnesses by offering them bribes, and the other for immoral conduct.

The *Carlow Sentinel* of 19 November finally published the full account of the inquiry, the findings of which were sensational. It was found that a member of McCaffrey's staff had attempted to bribe Mary Keefe's father to ask her to withdraw her allegations, while others tried to protect him by perjuring themselves. One witness in particular, a nurse called Catherine Corcoran, claimed to have witnessed Keefe having a relationship with a James Kerr, one of McCaffrey's keepers, and even claimed to have seen her having sex with Kerr at a clump of trees close to the asylum.

A few days later, the *Newry Telegraph* of Thursday, 24 November 1842, noted:

> the decision of his Excellency the Lord Lieutenant has been officially transmitted to the chairman of the Carlow Lunatic

> Asylum Board, and that it contains instructions for the immediate dismissal of Mr Patt McCaffrey, manager, John Moore and James Kerr – two of the keepers, and Catherine Corcoran, one of the nurses of the institution.

With regards to their treatment, two tables were presented showing the cure rates. The first was for those treated prior to March 1827, and detailed the numbers deemed to have 'mania' (or 'general insanity'), 'monomania' (or 'partial insanity'), 'dementia' (or 'fatuity'), and 'idiotism':

			Cured	Relieved	Died	Remain
Mania	Men	26	6	0	2	18
	Women	22	6	1	1	14
Monomania	Men	46	2	2	2	40
	Women	63	8	0	4	51
Dementia	Men	37	0	3	3	31
	Women	30	0	0	2	28
Idiotism	Men	18	0	0	1	17
	Women	15	0	0	3	12

The second was for those received at the asylum since March 1827:

			Cured	Relieved	Died	Remain
Mania	Men	16	7	1	2	6
	Women	10	6	1	0	3
Monomania	Men	23	12	2	0	9
	Women	50	25	1	0	24
Dementia	Men	9	0	1	4	4
	Women	2	0	0	1	1
Idiotism	Men	4	0	1	0	3
	Women	2	0	0	0	2
Improper	Men	4	0	0	0	0
	Women	1	0	0	0	0

The report was authored by Dr Osborne, the institution's physician, who then discussed some of the more barbaric treatments that had previously been employed by physicians to treat mental health issues, which he was advocating against the use of:

> one fact, however, cannot be too strongly impressed, that of the 72 successful cases, with one only was the lancet used. That bleeding is sometimes necessary, I am ready to admit, but I fear it has been too indiscriminately employed. Insanity frequently derives its origin from debility and exhaustion, when it is accompanied by restlessness, violence, and fury, and when the causes *prima facie* do not seem calculated for their production. To bleed a madman merely with a view to repress his fury, will be found futile, as he often becomes more violent after the operation, and many instances of curable mania will be caused to degenerate, by this debilitating practice, into confirmed fatuity.

(*Cork Constitution* (1828). Cork Lunatic Asylum. Saturday, 22 March. p.4. **www.britishnewspaperarchive.co.uk:** accessed 30 October 2024)

For the causes of the twenty-five deaths recorded over the previous year, Osborne offered the following explanations:

> Four were hapless idiots, one of whom was admitted in 1792, three died of pulmonary consumption – two of dropsy – four far advanced in life, who had long been insane from dysentery, which when it attacks aged maniacs is often fatal – four others equally advanced in years and insanity, sunk without bodily disease from general debility, the effect of long continued delirium; two cases died shortly after admission, exhausted by the violence of their disorder – four were sent in paralytic in such a state of helplessness, that the backs of two were ulcerated from the continued pressure of lying. An epileptic lunatic died suddenly and one man hanged himself. Unwearied perseverance is often exerted to accomplish self-destruction, – For five years this man's mind was intently fixed on it, his many attempts were however rendered abortive from the strict watch kept on him, but he at length succeeded. Tearing a night strip off his blanket, he passed it through the grating in his cell-door, scarcely five feet from the ground, and and was found in the morning dead, suspended in a sitting posture. Cases equally perverse and wayward are unfortunately numerous in all large establishments; they are painful and distressing to witness,

and require every effort of ingenuity and vigilance to counteract. (Ibid.)

The Criminal Lunatics (Ireland) Act of 1838 added pressure to the system, with individuals now able to be locked up in an asylum, if two magistrates and a physician decided that they were dangerous and likely to commit a crime. From 1868, all such cases were committed to asylums, rather than prison, significantly adding to the burden of the district system.

For the more serious cases, a 'Central Asylum for Insane Persons charged with Offences in Ireland' was facilitated by an Act of Parliament in 1845, and opened in 1850 as the Central Mental Hospital at Dundrum. This Victorian institution continued functioning until 2022, when its work and patients were transferred to a more modern facility on the site of St Ita's Hospital in Portrane.

As with hospital records, the medical records from Irish asylums are unfortunately not easy to access. Some of those in the Republic are deposited at the NAI, while others may be found in county archives, for example, those from Limerick Asylum are held by Limerick Archives. Permission is required from the original institution in advance to be able to consult them, which is often only given for academic purposes, with guidance again available from the NAI at **www.nationalarchives.ie/ article/guide-hospital-records/**.

For Northern Ireland, most records are also held at PRONI, with records closed for a hundred years after the date of the last entry in a particular register.

For the history of the asylum system in Ireland, Melinda D. Grimley-Smith's 2011 dissertation 'Politics, Professionalization, and Poverty: Lunatic Asylums for the Poor in Ireland, 1817–1920' is available via the Internet Archive at **https://web.archive.org/web/20220919060955id_/ https://curate.nd.edu/downloads/1831cj84d4c**, while Alice Mauger's *The Cost of Insanity in Nineteenth-Century Ireland: Public Voluntary and Private Asylum Care* (Palgrave MacMillan, 2018) offers further detailed insight.

Chapter 5

THEM AND US

There were several periods within the history of Ireland where the political aspirations of the people did not necessarily match those of the state or its many agencies. As a consequence, much hardship has been inflicted across the centuries, and a great deal of pain endured.

For centuries Ireland existed as an island and country which had a sense of itself and culture which conflicted with the views of the English, and then British, monarchs and governments that had laid claim to the island from the twelfth century. Much of the turmoil within Ireland within the modern period traces its origins back to the aftermath of the religious upheaval in England following the Reformation, the policies of plantation across the island of Ireland (particularly in Ulster), and the political chaos of the Wars of the Three Kingdoms, including the brutal Cromwellian conquest of the mid-seventeenth century.

In this section I will take a look at some of the more noticeable periods from the sixteenth century onwards, and how to pursue some of the relevant records of those caught up in the crossfires.

The Plantations of Ulster
Despite most Irish inhabitants being Roman Catholic, the Anglican based Church of Ireland was confirmed as the state church by the Act of Supremacy of 1558. Following rebellions against its rule in the 1580s, the English Crown again tried a plantation scheme in the province of Munster, following on from earlier attempts in counties Laois and Offaly in the 1530s. Some 3,000 settlers were this time sent to defend a million acres of land, but they were dispossessed of their holdings during the Nine Years' War of 1594–1603. This uprising against English rule was led by the Gaelic Irish chiefs Hugh O'Neill of Tyrone and Red Hugh O'Donnell of Tyrconnell, which soon collapsed thanks to a retaliatory military campaign

that devastated much of Ireland. On 4 September 1607 Hugh O'Neill, Rory O'Donnell, and ninety followers, set sail for Spain in the hopes of raising an army with which to return to finish off the job they had started in their previous campaign. This 'Flight of the Earls' was immediately followed by their lands being declared forfeit by the Crown.

In the peace that followed, the first successful Scottish colonisation attempt was made by two lairds, Hugh Montgomery and James Hamilton, who managed to obtain a large portion of County Down and a small part of County Antrim, commencing a settlement there of Scots in 1606. This settlement was encouraged by the new 'British' Crown, following the recent convergence of the royal lines of Scotland and England at the Union of the Crowns in 1603. With Elizabeth I having died without an heir, the Scottish king James VI had been invited to take the throne of England, and in doing so became James I of Great Britain. Concerned that Ulster was still the thorniest part of Ireland to contend with, the new king soon grabbed an opportunity to launch the largest colonisation scheme yet by a British monarch.

Three quarters of lands held by Irish landholders in the counties of Coleraine (now part of County Londonderry), Tyrconnell (now Donegal), Tyrone, Fermanagh, Armagh and Cavan were confiscated and distributed to Scots and English settlers, known as 'undertakers' and 'servitors', as well as to some 'deserving Irish' inhabitants deemed to be loyal. The land was granted to the undertakers in 'fee simple' (outright ownership), which could then be parcelled out further by them to tenants in 'fee farm'.

To finance this 'Plantation of Ulster', The Honourable The Irish Society was formed in London, which in 1610 was given the town of Derry to develop, with work then commencing in 1613 to transform it into the first planned city in Ireland. To reflect the London livery companies' funding, it was renamed 'Londonderry' and granted a royal charter. Although some towns had been created in Ireland in the medieval period long before the Plantations, such as Carrickfergus, Downpatrick and Cavan, a further forty towns were granted charters of incorporation, half of them within Ulster, to help urbanise the country and to encourage trade. These newly incorporated towns could also send elected members to the Irish Parliament in Dublin.

Although the Scots were invited to participate, this project was very much based on the power of the English in Ireland, with Scotland still a distinct, independent nation from England. Scottish undertakers wishing to participate therefore had to seek letters of denization or grants of naturalisation from the newly created British Crown (following the Union of the Crowns in 1603), to protect their property rights in Ireland through English law as loyal subjects.

> **TIP:** A list of the principal undertakers of the Ulster plantation is available at **www.ulsterancestry.com/free/ShowFreePage-335.html**.
>
> Findmypast also has a database entitled 'Britain and Ireland, Naturalisations 1603–1700', with material taken from the volume 'Letters of Denization and Acts of Naturalization for Aliens in England and Ireland, 1603–1700', edited by William A. Shaw, and published by The Huguenot Society of London in 1911. A typical example of a search from 1610 within this reveals the names of many Scots who sought denizen status in Ireland. In the bill 7 Jac I. No. 64, passed on 10 July 1610, we see that George Montgomery, Bishop of Derry, and Sir James Fullarton, both from Scotland, and both of the King's Council of Estate there, received denization status, as did Sir Hugh Montgomery, and his two sons, Hugh and James Montgomery, all of them Scottish.
>
> For more on denization and naturalisation under English and British law consult the UK National Archives guide 'Naturalisation, registration, and British citizenship' at **www.nationalarchives.gov.uk/help-with-your-research/research-guides/naturalisation-british-citizenship/**.
>
> The Ulster Historical Foundation (p.27) offers many publications and resources detailing aspects of the plantations.

The 1641 Rebellion

In 1641 a rebellion was instigated by Catholic gentry, many of them from Ulster, seeking to reclaim lands that had been taken from them during the recent plantations, and to reverse the discriminations being imposed upon them. As part of the uprising, hundreds of Protestants were massacred, including the murder of a hundred Protestants at Portadown by Irish rebels. In retaliation, many Catholics were also murdered by Protestant settlers, including an incident where between twenty and thirty Catholics in the County Antrim parish of Islandmagee were murdered. To help suppress the Irish uprising, a Scottish Covenanting army arrived in 1642, causing further mayhem.

A useful resource for those trying to connect ancestors to the 1641 Irish Rebellion is Trinity College Dublin's '1641 Depositions' project at **https://1641.tcd.ie**. This mainly provides statements gathered in five collections between 1641 and 1654 from Protestant settlers who witnessed the uprising, or who had property damaged, but also includes testimony from some Catholic witnesses. Statements were recorded across the four provinces. The original records have been digitised and can be viewed on the site, though with the difficult handwriting from the time you may wish to use the equally accessible transcripts.

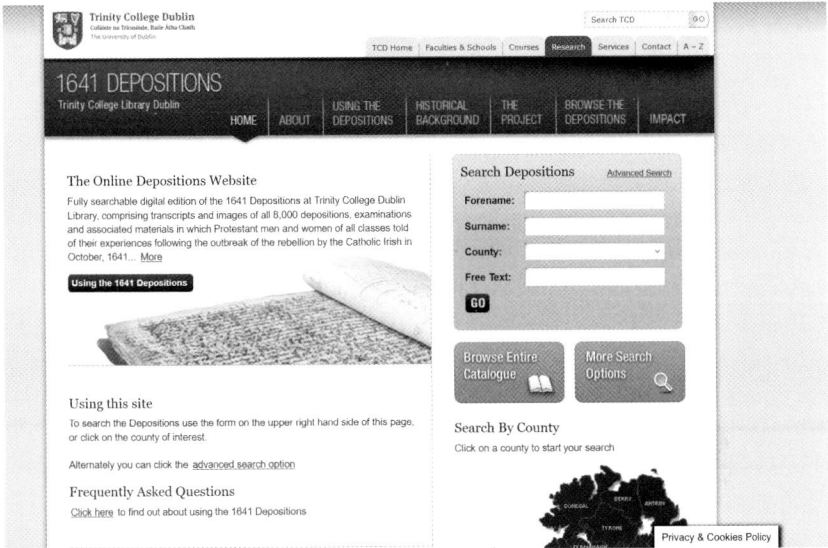

The 1641 Depositions website from Trinity College Dublin offers access to 8,000 depositions recorded in the aftermath of the atrocities.

CASE STUDY: My Brown ancestors, from Islandmagee in Co. Antrim, can be traced with certainty there back to about 1762, but the family is documented on the peninsula right back to the start of the seventeenth century, with the earliest member being a Scot, Robert Brown, who died in the parish on 1 August 1657. Just four years earlier, details about both him and his son James make for sensational reading in the 1641 Depositions, with both alleged to have participated in the murder of many Roman Catholics there during the rebellion.

The first damning evidence against Robert Brown came from 28-year-old survivor Bryan Magee, who made the following statement at Lisnagarvy on 21 April 1653 about the murder of his family:

> about 8 January 1641 this Examinant then liuing in the Isle McGee in his ffathers howse Owen McGee in the nighte aboute bed time some knockt at the dore and this examinants mother opened the dore and there came in Robert Browne now living in the Isle McGee and his sonne James with there swords drawne and severall others of the Neighbours … and they killed at that time Jane Mother of this Examinant and Margaret O Carrell …

and Doltagh McGee a sucking Child brothers to this examinant and Margaret Mary and Mena sisters to this Examinant

(1641 Depositions, Ireland (1653). MAGEE, Bryan, 21 April. Trinity College Dublin. MS 838, fols 200r-201v. **https://1641.tcd.ie**: accessed 30 October 2024)

Bryan Magee escaped the slaughter with his father, and brothers Henry and Turlough, and hid for an hour, before being joined by Bryan Boy Magee from a neighbouring house and others, where a similar murder had also occurred by the Scots. All set off for Carrickfergus to seek the protection of the colonel in the castle, but when they arrived, the colonel was not there, and several soldiers on duty duly killed Bryan Boy Magee, as well as Bryan's father and brothers, although Bryan Magee again managed to escape.

When quizzed about his involvement on 27 May 1653, the following deposition concerning Robert Brown was recorded:

who being demanded where he was that night when Donell McArt Magee & his family & then rest of the families were kild in Isle Magee saith he was in his house all that night & his wife & children & his servants Rob: Orr John Hunter & Agnes Woodside & Marren Carr & saith that his eldest sonne Hugh Browne was Lieut: to Capten McCulloghes company in Carrickfergus & saith that the morning before in the Sabbath day he had sent his sonne Hugh James to his brother James Hugh to see how he did & that he did not returne home till about between eleven or twelve a clock that night at which time this examinant & his said family were in bed & that his said sonne James came to his bed syde & told him that his brother Hugh was well And being demanded whether his said sone James told him of any stirr that was in or about the way as he came home saith he did not relate any such thing to him that night And further saith that he understood from him the next morning that the reason of his staying out soe long out that night was because he had mett some company & fell to drink with them in one John McGeughes house in the Scotch quarter without the gate of Carrickfergus And further saith that when he was told in the morning of the killing of those persons he did not inquire who did it nor did he then heare though the said

Donell McArts Magees house was very neare this examinants house & within less then a Muskett shott.

(1641 Depositions, Ireland (1653). BROWN, Robt. 27 May. Trinity College Dublin. MS 838, fols 310r-311v. **https://1641.tcd.ie**: accessed 30 October 2024)

A further deposition from a James Collogh on 1 June 1653 also provides details about Robert's wife, naming her as Jennett Woodsyde, and the fact that it seems Robert was held prisoner for a time in Carrickfergus:

at the tyme of the Massacre in the Isle of Magee he this examinant was capten of a foot company in this towne under in the Regiment of Collonell Chichester, and that shortely after the sayd massacre, one Jennett Woodsyde wife to Robert Browne now prisoner in this towne told this examinant that one Robert Glasgow did kill Tieg o Sheale with a shot of a horsemans peece and that one commonly called Stagg fferry was at the house of Donnell McArt and as she heard killed his wife; And being asked what he could tell concerning the murder of Owen Modder Magee Henry Magee & Bryan Magee neere vnto this towne he this examinant saith that at the tyme the sayd murder was acted he was asleepe vpon a bed and cannott tell who was the actors in the sayd murder otherwise them that he was told that Lieutenant William Dawbyn doeth acknowledge himselfe to haue had a hand therein, and that he would Justifye the same for that he did it by order and this examinant sayth that the reason of his knowledg is, for that one John McClowy who was then Corporall to this examinant the sayd Lieutenant Dawbyn told him soe and further saith not.

(1641 Depositions, Ireland (1653). COLLOGH, James. 1 June. Trinity College Dublin. MS 838, fols 208r-209v. **https://1641.tcd.ie**: accessed 30 October 2024)

It seems that Robert and James, who was also a prisoner, were subsequently set free.

The Cromwellian Conquest

The Catholic rebellion in Ireland was finally crushed during the Cromwellian conquest of 1649–1653, which included the controversial massacre of Catholic Confederate and English Royalist troops, as well as many civilians, at the Siege of Drogheda in 1649.

In 1652 the English Parliament's Act of Settlement decreed which lands in Ireland were to be forfeited by Catholic landowners who had participated in the 1641 rebellion, as well as those of Catholic clergy, royalists and anyone who had directed hostilities against the English army during the Wars of the Three Kingdoms. The intent was to convey their holdings to loyal English soldiers for service and to 'adventurers' or speculators for their investment in the conflict, with many of the dispossessed Catholics affected forcibly transplanted to the province of Connacht. Catholics were also banned from holding office in the Irish Parliament.

To prepare for the mass forfeiture, Cromwell ordered a Civil Survey to be carried out from 1654 to 1656 to value land across the four provinces (although most of Connacht had already been surveyed in an earlier exercise from 1630). With the aid of this information, Sir William Petty was tasked with carrying out the more accurate Down Survey from 1656 to 1658. The survey, and the accompanying maps generated, were the first attempt to accurately map the island of Ireland, with the map recorded at a scale of forty perches to the inch.

The Down Survey website at **https://downsurvey.tchpc.tcd.ie** can be used to trace the change in land ownership between 1641 and 1670, as noted in the Books of Survey and Distribution. Various published volumes of the Books of Survey and Distribution, and from the earlier Civil Survey, can be accessed in digital format also via the Irish Manuscripts Commission website (p.9).

The Penal Laws

The implementation of the Penal Laws against both Roman Catholics and Presbyterians, particularly in the aftermath of the so-called 'Glorious Revolution' of 1688–1689, soon led to the creation of an Anglo-Irish-dominated Protestant establishment known as the Ascendancy. Consequently, many Presbyterians from Ulster emigrated to the American colonies (where they became known as the 'Scotch-Irish'), while those who remained behind were discriminated against, although not to the same degree as the Roman Catholic population.

Various discriminatory laws were implemented, including acts in 1704 to register Catholic priests and to deny Catholics the right to inherit land from Protestants, or to buy land; their own lands were also to be divided equally among all surviving sons after death, rather than by a single heir, unless the eldest son had converted to Protestantism. The 1727 Disenfranchising Act blocked Catholics from voting in parliamentary elections (a right not returned until 1793), while Presbyterian marriages were not legally recognised. Intermarriage between Catholics and Protestants was also forbidden. A good outline of the Penal Laws can be read at **https://macmillan.yale.edu/glc/history-penal-laws-against-irish-catholics**, as drawn from Sir Henry Parnell's *A History of the Penal Laws Against the Irish Catholics, Fourth Edition* (1825, London).

With the threat of Jacobitism receding in the latter part of the eighteenth century, many of the laws were gradually withdrawn, with the Catholic Relief Act of 1793 the first major milestone. However, it was not until Ireland's entry into the United Kingdom in 1801, that moves to remove the remaining Penal Laws were introduced, with full Catholic emancipation finally occurring in 1829.

> **TIP:** One way for Roman Catholics to remove themselves from the hardships of the Penal laws was to convert to the state church, the Church of Ireland. In 1774, it became possible for Catholics to swear an oath of loyalty to the Crown at the local assizes, with the declarations then recorded in the Catholic Qualification Rolls.
>
> These rolls can be searched from 1700 to 1845 via the NAI records platform at **http://census.nationalarchives.ie/search/cq/home.jsp**. The style of the registers change across time, but typical entries will note the name of the person converting, the county of residence, the date of the oath, and when enrolled. In some cases the townland of residence may also be included, as may occupations.

The Great Famine

Ireland was forced into a union with Britain in the aftermath of the failed United Irishmen rebellion of 1798, with the new 'United Kingdom of Great Britain and Ireland' coming into legal force from 1 January 1801. For some the union brought prosperity, for others it was deeply resented and agitated against throughout the nineteenth century.

The biggest ever catastrophe in Ireland's history occurred less than half a century later, between 1845 and 1851. The Great Famine, known in Irish as 'An Gorta Mór', followed the failure of the potato crop, a key staple of diet for the very poorest in society. During the crisis the workhouses of Ireland were completely overwhelmed, and over a million people died,

A replica of the tall ship **Jeanie Johnston**, *can be visited on the River Liffey in Dublin. The original vessel made 16 crossings from 1848 to 1855 to Canada, taking some 2,500 emigrants from Ireland.*

many of them buried in 'famine pits'. A further million were forced to emigrate, creating much of the worldwide diaspora that exists to this day. Most travelled to Britain, North America and Australia, although many died en route in the overcrowded 'coffin ships' used by many shipping firms to transport them. So great were the numbers arriving in Canada in 1847 that the UK heavily restricted Irish access into the country, forcing many of the refugees to make for the US instead. As a consequence, large Irish populations were established in Boston, Chicago and Toronto, among other cities.

The Famine Memorial on Custom House Quay, Dublin.

The Famine itself is too large a topic for this book, but the background to the catastrophe is outlined on Wesley Johnston's site at **www.wesleyjohnston.com/users/ireland/past/famine/index.htm**, while the Irish government and University College Cork have produced The Great Irish Famine Online at **www.irishfamine.ie/greatirishfamineonline**, to provide access to interactive maps which detail how the crisis affected people across the country.

In November 1845 the Famine Relief Commission was established, continuing its work until February 1847 (with a brief interruption), to oversee relief efforts and to provide means to feed those affected through soup kitchens and by other means. Digitised images from the body can be accessed on Ancestry through its 'Ireland, Famine Relief Commission Papers 1844–1847' database, the records having been soured from the NAI. Additional research materials that can help include surviving workhouse registers and boards of guardians minutes, as well as vestry records of the Church of Ireland (p.89).

> **TIP:** The 1851 census in Britain, available on all major commercial genealogy platforms, can be used to trace those who crossed the Irish Sea, but bear in mind most records will simply note the birthplace of an Irish immigrant as 'Ireland', at times making it difficult to confirm if you have the right individual. The poor law application records in English, Welsh and Scottish based county archives may also include entries of those arriving in Britain to seek relief, with universal poor relief measures having commenced in England and Wales in 1834, and in Scotland in 1845.

Following the Famine, many landowners suffered from a loss of income from tenants and devaluation of their land, forcing many towards bankruptcy. Many were trapped within their own aristocratic establishments, unable to sell their estates due to them being 'encumbered' with obligations to pay set amounts to family members as part of marriage settlements, and previous provisions as set out in wills and entails prior to its inheritance.

The Encumbered Estates Acts of 1848 and 1849 allowed landowners to free themselves from these burdens, by selling their estates to the state, which could then redistribute them to new owners with a new title granted, clear of any previous burdens or debts. The courts evolved into the Land Judges Court in 1872. As part of the sales processes, catalogues were drawn up for each estate, which included details of the rentals of properties present with them. These can be searched on Findmypast's 'Landed Estates Court Rentals 1850–1885' database, also available on FamilySearch in a collection of the same name.

The Land War

In 1879 the Land War then exploded in Ireland, with the main issues being how to address the parasitical nature of landlordism, with demands for fair rent, better security of tenure, and an improved right to buy. Many instances of hardship by tenants are documented in the press of the time, with a good example in the following case study.

> **CASE STUDY**: The following case concerning the extortionate rent being paid by a member of my wife's family was raised at a meeting of an arbitration scheme in Carrick-on-Suir, Co. Tipperary, in June 1888, as reported in *The County Tipperary Independent and Tipperary Free Press* of 9 June 1888 (Carrick-on-Suir: the New Arbitration Scheme, p.8):
>
> A case has turned up in our district – that of Mrs Prendergast, of Killonerry. The woman has 15 acres of land, and has paid for the past 50 years the enormous sum of £3,000 …. She would continue to pay it if she had it, or could borrow it. Some people appear to have an objection to amicable settlements between landlord and tenant. Now, my neighbours, I wish that someone – no matter if he were a Hottentot – would see justice done to Mrs Prendergast. Cardinal Moran once said that in some cases the landlords ought to be made make restitution to their tenants for the unjust rents exacted from them. I believe that by Cardinal Moran, or any equity court in the world, this case would be considered one of plain robbery (hear, hear). The Rev. Chairman concluded by exhorting them to stick to the fight and never to recede from their present position until justice was done.

In response to the situation, the British government passed the Land Law (Ireland) Act 1881 to establish a new Irish Land Commission, which initially sought to intervene in the rents issue, but which also assumed the work of the Landed Estates courts. The commission also took on the role of a tenancy purchasing commission, assisting those wishing to buy their holdings outright with loans to be repaid over thirty-five years at 5 per cent interest, and granting tenants 'vesting orders' for their new holdings, essentially title deeds in their name, clear of any previous burdens or encumbrances. The scheme was further extended with the Purchase of Land (Ireland) Act in 1885, which extended loans repayments to over forty-nine years, and again in 1889.

The Findmypast database 'Ireland, Land Commission Advances, 1891–1920' details many of those who applied and received loans as a part of the scheme.

The Home Rule Crisis

As the land issue rolled on, the predominant political issue of the late nineteenth and early twentieth centuries became that of Home Rule, namely the question of how Ireland should be governed within the United Kingdom – either through direct rule from the Westminster-based Parliament in England, or via a devolved Parliament in Ireland. As pressure for Home Rule increased, the Ulster Unionist Council was formed in 1905 to oppose it, bringing together interested parties from across Ulster's nine counties, including delegates from the Orange Order, elected officials, peers and Unionist associations.

On 11 April 1912 the Liberal government introduced legislation for a third Home Rule Bill, something long feared by the majority of the Protestant Unionist population. A protest against the devolution plans was held on 28 September 1912, designated as 'Ulster Day' by the Ulster Unionist Council. Unionists recorded their outrage in ink, with some 237,368 men signing a document called the 'Ulster Covenant', and a further 234,046 women signing an equivalent 'Declaration of Loyalty'.

The signatures of those who signed the Covenant have been digitised and made available online by PRONI at **www.nidirect.gov.uk/services/search-ulster-covenant**. The document is searchable by surname, forename, address, parliamentary division, district, place of signing, and even by the name of the agent gathering the signatures at each location. Ancestry also offers access through its third party 'Web: Ulster, Ireland, Ulster Covenant, 1912' database.

> **TIP:** When searching the Covenant, if you find a person at a particular address, it is worth doing a second search on the address itself, as many others resident within the same household might have signed it also.

As a consequence of the Home Rule issue, two militias were established in Ireland, almost taking the country to civil war. The Ulster Volunteer Force (UVF) was an armed volunteer militia of more than 100,000 men, officially formed by the Ulster Unionist Council on 13 January 1913, and led by Edward Carson and James Craig, its aim to oppose the implementation of devolution. In response to its creation came a parallel organisation, the Nationalist based Irish Volunteers, formed in November 1913 by the Irish Republican Brotherhood (IRB) with an opposing remit to defend any forthcoming Home Rule settlement. Control of this organisation soon passed to John Redmond of the Irish Parliamentary Party, who was determined that the movement would not try to disrupt the flow of the Home Rule Bill in Parliament.

The Ulster Unionist Council Papers, covering the period from 1800 to 1992, are catalogued under D1327, with a guide to the holdings contained within available at **www.bit.ly/UlsterUnionistCouncil**. They include a wealth of material relating to the UVF, including minutes of the Co. Down Committee of the UVF from 1912 to 1915; Headquarters' Council minutes from 1914 to 1920, material on gun-running efforts at Larne, Bangor and Donaghadee in April 1914, and many photographs of various UVF reviews and parades from the period. In addition, the collection contains records for many Ulster Unionist associations, from which members were drawn, while a range of UVF recruitment lists and papers also exist at the facility – for example for Seaford Company, County Down (D1263/3), the 2nd Battalion North Derry (D304/1; the collection also includes two armbands worn by UVF volunteers), 1st Battalion Armagh (D1966), Lisburn (D845/4), Cookstown (D1132), and a list for County Fermanagh (D1402/3/1). Documents concerning UVF members are also included within the files gathered by the British administration in Dublin Castle. Records for the Ulster Women's Unionist Council are further catalogued at PRONI under D1098, with a useful article on its formation available at **https://tinyurl.com/UlsterWomensUnionistCouncil**.

Records for the Irish Volunteers can be located in many archives and libraries. Papers of Galway City Corps from 1914, for example, are held

> **TIP:** While it is difficult to work out who may have had membership of either militia, thousands of members signed up to the British Army upon the declaration of war against Germany in 1914. Signing up to the British Army at this time does not confirm previous membership, but may be a strong indicator that the applicant had previous UVF or Irish Volunteers connections.

at Galway County Council Archives (under GCCA/GS01/02–03), with some digitised and made available via its website at **www.galway.ie/digitalarchives**. Membership lists for Cork, 1913–1914, are available at Cork City and County Archives via **https://tinyurl.com/CorkVolunteers**.

The Suffragettes

Many different groups campaigned for women's votes across Ireland from the late nineteenth century and up to the First World War. In 1872 the North of Ireland Women's Suffrage Society (NIWSS) was formed by Isabella Tod. This was followed by the Dublin Women's Suffrage Society in 1874, which was later renamed in 1898 as the Irish Women's Suffrage and Local Government Association (IWSLGA). Its driving force was Anna Haslam.

The first militant actions in pursuit of the vote took place in Ireland in 1908, by the Irish Women's Franchise League (IWFL), which believed that the IWSLGA was achieving too little, too slowly. In 1909, the NIWSS, now with some 3,000 members across the North, changed its name to the Irish Women's Suffrage Society (IWSS). Two of its members were arrested in London two years later for civil disobedience.

Other groups to emerge included the Munster Women's Franchise League, with strong support in Cork, Limerick and Waterford, and the Irish Women's Suffrage Foundation, led by Hannah Sheehy-Skeffington and Margaret Cousins. Soon the movement was disparagingly referred to as the Suffragettes, rather than Suffragists. The following resources can also help with Suffragette research in Ireland:

- Details of some female prisoners can be found in Findmypast's 'Irish Prison Registers 1790–1924' database (requires a subscription to see results).
- A timeline of events from the North, created by the Northern Irish Assembly, is online at **http://bit.ly/SuffragettetimelineNI**.
- An account of the Suffragettes in the North is available from **https://web.archive.org/web/20240226072032/http://www.belfasthistoryproject.com/thesuffragettes/**.
- The NAI hosts the free to access digitised 'Minute Book of the Dublin Women's Suffrage Association/Irish Woman's Suffrage and Local Government Association (1876–1913)' at **www.nationalarchives.ie/article/minute-book-dublin-womens-suffrage-association-irish-womens-suffrage-local-government-association-1876–1913/**.

An interesting tool online is the 'PRONI Suffrage Map' at **https://dfcgis. maps.arcgis.com/apps/MapSeries/index.html?appid= 58d83b0ec9ce4c60be299bfa12780c77**, which plots various incidents which occurred in Belfast (and one in Derry/Londonderry). Each site numbered on the map of Belfast has an accompany tab which relates information about the incident in question, as sourced from the British Newspaper Archive.

> **TIP:** In May 1912 the *Irish Citizen* newspaper was established with Hannah Sheehy-Skeffington as its editor. Coverage from this paper between 25 May 1912 and 2 August 1920 can be found on the British Newspaper Archive, along with contemporary coverage of Suffragette incidents in other Irish and British based titles.

The Dublin Lockout

The Dublin Lockout was a bitter workers' rights struggle that lasted from 26 August 1913 to 18 January 1914, which involved some 20,000 workers in disputes with over 300 firms. At the heart of the strike was the battle for workers to be allowed to unionise.

In 1909, Liverpool-born trade unionist 'Big' Jim Larkin established the Irish Transport and General Workers Union (ITGWU) in 1909, to try to improve the lot of the ordinary working man in Ireland, in a country riddled with poverty and high rates of disease in the city slums. A parallel body was also set up in September 1911 for women by Larkin, with the assistance of his sister Delia, called the Irish Women's Workers' Union (IWWU). In 1911, Larkin also established the Irish Labour Party with James Connolly.

On 13 August 1913, the chairman of the Dublin United Tramway Company, William Martin Murphy, sacked fifty tram workers for belonging to the Irish Transport and General Workers Union (ITGWU), which had been formed four years earlier by Jim Larkin. Another 300 workers were dismissed a week later. On the morning of 26 August, tram workers within the union retaliated by going out on strike to protest, with the action soon spreading to other industries.

In response to the strike, sympathetic employers to Murphy responded with a lockout, and brought 'scab' labour over from Britain to fill the positions of the striking workers. On 30 August, the situation deteriorated further when, after a planned rally by Larkin at the ITGWU headquarters was banned, two protesting strikers were killed in a police baton charge on Sackville Street (now O'Connell Street). Over the next

> **CASE STUDY:** One of the tram workers who went on strike on 26 August was my three times great-uncle, Alexander William Halliday (p.48), who was subsequently tried at the Southern Police Court on 23 September 1913 for abandoning his tram in Dublin city centre. Alexander was prosecuted alongside nine other tram car drivers, and fifteen conductors, with the prosecution covered in the *Daily Dublin News*:
>
> The presiding magistrate, Mr Drury, noted the following in summing up:
>
> > These men should understand that to leave their cars without notice in the streets was a great offence against the company and also a great offence against the public. They had no right to turn out like that and leave the cars in the streets. They were liable to fines of 40s, but he thought justice would be met by fines of 5s, which should be paid within a week.
>
> (*Daily Dublin News* (1913). Leaving Trams on the Street. 24 September. p.6. **www.britishnewspaperarchive.co.uk**: accessed on 30 October 2024)
>
> Alexander does not appear to have joined the Irish Citizen's Army, and spent the rest of his working life on the trams.

two days, ITGWU representatives James Connolly and Jim Larkin were arrested, and upon their release, the two gentlemen established a new defensive militia force, the Irish Citizen Army, armed with hurleys to ward off further attacks by the Crown's forces.

The lockout continued until January of the following year, with much rioting and many casualties. Although the workers were eventually forced to return to work, many businesses were forced into bankruptcy over the dispute.

Various resources can help to research the dispute, although the records of the ITGWU were unfortunately destroyed in 1916:

- The Dublin Metropolitan Police's Prisoners Books from 1911 to 1918 cover the period of the Lockout, and can be found at **https://digital.ucd.ie/view/ucdlib:43945**, with each volume including a name index. James Connolly's and James Larkin's arrests on 30 and 31 August 1913, for example, are found on p.227 in Book 3

(1911–1913), with the charge for both being 'incitement to crime', and the relevant sentences recorded. A third party index to the books, which can be easier to use, is available via Findmypast's 'Ireland, Dublin Metropolitan Police Prisoners Books 1905–1908 and 1911–1918' collection.

- The NLI's manuscript collections at **http://catalogue.nli.ie** holds many documents concerning the Irish Citizen Army, such as those gathered by Labour Party leader William O'Brien, including roll books, members lists, articles, correspondence, pamphlets and circulars, many of which have been digitised (catalogued under MS 15,673). Other notebooks, pamphlets and bulletins are also available, with many digitised and available online.
- The NLI hosts an exhibition about the Lockout at **www.nli.ie/lockout**, which contains an interactive map detailing key locations in Dublin where events took place, as well as video interviews with archivists and historians on its importance and legacy.
- A defunct site examining the same events has been cached by the Internet Archive at **https://tinyurl.com/1913Lockout**, with several background essays, biographies on key personnel, podcasts, videos and more.

The First World War

With the outbreak of the First World War, the implementation of Home Rule was suspended. Members of the Nationalist based Irish Volunteers were encouraged to join the British Army, to defend the progress made so far. Subsequently, 140,000 enlisted, becoming known as the 'National Volunteers', with about 24,000 of them serving with the 10th and 16th (Irish) divisions in the British Army. A smaller element of the movement refused to enlist, however, and continued as the more militant wing of the Irish Volunteers, later to play a crucial part within the Easter Rising of 1916 (p.142). Members of the Protestant based Ulster Volunteer Force also enlisted with the British Army as the 36th (Ulster) Division, expecting their loyalty to be rewarded with the abolition of Home Rule altogether.

There are many resources available on the large commercial genealogy vendor sites to research those who enlisted, including service records (of which only a third have survived), medal index cards, Silver War Badge recipients (for those who were injured), war diaries, and considerably more. Guides to various British Army records collections are available on the UK National Archives platform at **www.nationalarchives.gov.**

uk/help-with-your-research/research-guides/. In addition to the British Army, many Irish people served with the Royal Navy, with additional guides to these available on the platform.

CASE STUDY: Martin Colleton was born on 7 September 1883 at Greystone Street, Carrick-on-Suir. On 22 October 1902 he joined the Connaught Rangers, with his enlistment record noting that he was 5ft 3½in, 116lb in weight, and with a fresh complexion, blue eyes and light brown hair, and a scar on the palm of his right hand extending to the middle of his index finger.

For the first two years of service, Martin was based in Ireland, but regularly fell into trouble with his regiment; for example, on 1 May 1903, he was arrested after creating a disturbance in the town of Mullingar after a little too much to drink, and confined to barracks for ten days. On 31 October 1903, Martin went absent without leave, returning to his home town of Carrick-on-Suir, where he was subsequently arrested by the civil police and returned to Mullingar, with another ten days confined to barracks.

In October 1904 Martin was posted to the Indian town of Ahmednagar, near Bombay, where he spent the next six years, his service record again littered with prosecutions for being absent without leave, and drinking. His most serious misdemeanour was on 25 December 1907, Christmas Day, when he deserted his post early when supposed to be acting as a sentinel. After being found guilty at a court-martial, he received a sentence of fifty-six days detention.

Martin was transferred back to Ireland in January 1911, where he became a special reservist, a position due to expire on 21 October 1914. However, with the outbreak of war, he re-engaged with the Connaught Rangers at Pontypridd in Wales, and was sent to France to join the rest of the 2nd Battalion as part of the original British Expeditionary Force. Going over the top from the waterlogged, muddy, bloody trenches at Ypres, Martin's war was to tragically end, as he was mowed down by enemy fire. His body was never recovered, and he is today remembered with nearly 55,000 other missing British troops at the Menin Gate Memorial.

Shortly after Martin's death, two of his brothers would form a different relationship with the British Army, taking up arms against it for the republican cause, with brother John joining the Irish Republican Army, and his brother Patrick instructing the republican youth wing, Na Fianna Éireann.

Simon Fowler's *Tracing Your First World War Ancestors: A Guide for Family Historians*, is a further helpful resource.

The Easter Rising

Believing that 'England's difficulty was Ireland's opportunity', on 24 April, Easter Monday, over a thousand Irish Volunteers and associates, including the Irish Citizen Army, launched an uprising against British rule that would become known as the 'Easter Rising'. They stormed several buildings and areas, including the General Post Office (GPO), Phoenix Park, Dublin Castle, buildings surrounding military barracks at Beggars Bush, the South Dublin Union workhouse, and other key locations in the city. Headquarters were established at the GPO, and from here Patrick Pearse read out the 'Proclamation of the Republic' on behalf of a new 'provisional government', while the Irish tricolour was raised over the building – displaying green and orange stripes to represent the two main political traditions of the island, separated by a white stripe for peace.

In response, the British administration hastily ordered troops in from surrounding training barracks, with reinforcements sent over by boat from England. For the next week the two forces fought a bloody campaign against each other on Dublin's streets, with over 500 fatalities, many of them civilians. As well as the British Army, the RIC and the DMP also countered the rebellion. For the names of the civilians and personnel killed, consult the 1916 Necrology at **https://web.archive.org/web/20201128121244/https:/**

Memorial to the volunteers from Clonmel in County Tipperary who mobilised during Easter Week in 1916.

www.glasnevintrust.ie/-uuid/55a29fab-3b24-41dd-a1d9-12d148a78f74/Glasnevin-Trust-1916–Necrology-485.pdf.

By the following Saturday, the rebel stronghold at the GPO had become untenable, and the order was given for the volunteers to surrender. Following the uprising, over 3,500 rebels were arrested, though most were soon released. The leaders, including Pearse and Connolly, were court-martialled and sentenced to death, with the executions happening at Kilmainham Gaol, Dublin. For a list of the leaders executed, visit **https://tinyurl.com/Executed1916Leaders**.

The Military Archives platform at **www.militaryarchives.ie** has a range of resources concerning those who served during the rebellion, including nominal rolls for the Irish Citizen Army and other Dublin brigades of the Irish Volunteers, as well as medal claims in its aftermath, following the creation of the Irish Free State from December 1922. There are also records for those who later claimed a military service pension for their participation in Dublin, and a list of confirmed veterans with a recognised role in the rebellion, including their names, addresses, locations and file references for further documentation. Searchable witness statements by survivors who participated in the rebellion, as gathered by the Bureau of Military History between 1947 and 1957, are also included on the platform.

Daily Dublin Metropolitan Police reports of the 'Movement of Extremists' between 29 May 1915 and 20 April 1916 have been catalogued by the NAI under CSO/JD/2, and made available at **www.nationalarchives.ie/article/chief-secretarys-office-crime-branch-dublin-metropolitan-police-dmp-movement-extremists-april-1916/**. The archive has also provided the Colonial Office (Irish Branch) 1916 Easter Rising Compensation Files, dating from 1917 to 1925 at **http://centenaries.nationalarchives.ie/centenaries/plic**. These documents relate to claims for damages to property sustained during the rebellion, as administered by the Property Losses (Ireland) Committee, later to become the Irish Branch of the UK's Colonial Office.

The UK's National Archives has many contemporary documents on the British administration of Ireland at the time, with a research guide available at **www.nationalarchives.gov.uk/help-with-your-research/research-guides/ireland-easter-rising-1916/**. The main collections are located under WO 35, WO 32, CO 903 and CO 904. Records include 171 court martial documents following the Rising, various Home Office lists of Irish prisoners in British gaols, intelligence reports within the Dublin Castle records, War Office records of civilians prosecuted, and records from a subsequent Royal Commission enquiring into the events of the rebellion (catalogued under HO 45/10810/312350 and PRO 30/67/31). A great number of the records are name searchable via the archive's Discovery catalogue at **http://discovery.nationalarchives.gov.uk**. For details of Irish folk who returned from Britain to participate in the Rising, visit **https://hiddenheroesofeasterweek.wordpress.com**.

Ancestry hosts some digitised records from CO 903, WO 35 and WO 71 within its 'Ireland, Courts Martial Files 1916–1922' collection, as well as profiles of those suspected by the Dublin Metropolitan Police and the Royal Irish Constabulary of being disloyal to the Crown in its 'Ireland, Intelligence Profiles, 1914–1922' database. Findmypast's 'Easter Rising & Ireland Under Martial Law 1916–1921' set has additional records from WO 35, WO 141 and HO 144 available, which note the names of civilians and soldiers court-martialled after the Rising, as well as further records for the subsequent War of Independence (see below).

The NLI has many contemporary resources. An overview of key events, including documents on the main participants, is available in a cached online exhibition at **www.bit.ly/NLI-2016**. The National Library also hosts an interesting online exhibition at **www.nli.ie/1916**, providing a broad overview of the key events.

The *Sinn Féin Rebellion Handbook* has been digitised and made available for free consultation at **https://archive.org/details/sinnfeinrebellio00dubl**, and also on Findmypast. This is a compendium of articles produced in 1917 covering the events of the Rising as reported by the *Weekly Irish Times*, which contains detailed lists of those involved, as well as coverage produced in the immediate aftermath of the rebellion.

The War of Independence

In the aftermath of the Easter Rising, various attitudes in Irish society began to change towards the idea of Irish independence. The executions of the rebellion's leaders at Kilmainham Gaol had appalled many, but it was to be the issue of forcible recruitment into the British Army that was to act as the catalyst for the growth of Sinn Féin.

In the North, by contrast, the dominant Unionist position in Ulster hardened, and demands for a partition of the island, first posited in 1914, began to grow. The conscription crisis of 1918 hardened the support of nationalist Ireland against the British state, with rallies held across the country to protest against its implementation.

In December 1918, Sinn Féin won 73 of 105 seats in the UK General Election – despite over 30 of their candidates having been interned in British jails, while the Unionists, mainly in Ulster, won 26 seats. Refusing to take up their seats in London, on 21 January 1919 Sinn Féin established a separate parliament, Dáil Éireann, which duly reaffirmed the nation's independence as proclaimed in 1916. In September, the British declared the *Dáil* to be illegal. On the same day as the Dáil convened, the War of Independence, also known as the Anglo-Irish War, commenced. This was a guerilla war fought by the 'Irish Republican Army' (IRA), a newly designated military force drawn from previous groups such as the Irish Volunteers and Irish Citizen Army, against the Royal Irish Constabulary, the Dublin Metropolitan Police, and to a lesser extent, the British Army. For membership details for many of those who served with the IRA can be determined from the Military Archives website. The Republican newspaper An tÓglach, considered to be the IRA's newspaper in the conflict, is also available to read on the platform.

The British deployed a new force to Ireland to support the police, called the Royal Irish Constabulary Special Reserve, drawn up from ex-service personnel who had just demobilised from the British Army. Recruited mostly from Britain, but with some Irish members, they became known as the 'Black and Tans', due to their uniform colours. Three months later, they were joined by another unit, the Royal Irish Constabulary Auxiliaries, a more extreme paramilitary group with membership drawn from former British Army officers, their role being to effect a more militant policy of counter-insurgency. They soon gained a reputation for brutality against both the IRA and civilians alike, although outrages were committed by both sides.

Service records for the RIC are available on Findmypast (p.17), but note that for War of Independence research, these include service records for the RIC Auxiliaries. A book entitled *Tales of the R.I.C* is also available on the Internet Archive at **https://archive.org/details/talesofric00edinuoft**, and covers the period of the War of Independence up to the truce in 1921.

During the conflict Ireland was partitioned by the British government, through the Government of Ireland Act 1920, into two territories, Northern Ireland and Southern Ireland, with each to have its own respective Parliament as devolved legislatures of the United Kingdom. The Northern Irish Parliament was established at Stormont in May 1921, but Sinn Féin boycotted the Parliament of Southern Ireland and instead continued to sit in government from August 1921 as the Second *Dáil* Éireann.

While many incidents and outrages in the post-Partition period are documented in the press, in the new state of Northern Ireland the press was largely Unionist, with its own perception on proceedings happening in the North. A publication entitled *Facts and Figures of the Belfast Pogrom 1920–1922* was commissioned by Michael Collins to provide a counter-perspective to the press's description of hostilities against the Catholic community of Belfast, but due to the fragile politics between the two new states, it was never published at the time. It finally saw publication in 1997 (see appendix).

The Treaty and the Civil War

In July, with both sides approaching a military stalemate, an official truce was agreed between the British government and the IRA. This led to the signing of the Anglo-Irish Treaty on 6 December 1921, which granted Southern Ireland dominion status within the British Empire as a new 'Irish Free State' (Saorstát Éireann) from 6 December 1922, but which confirmed the Partition of the island.

Although the Treaty was ratified by the Second *Dáil*, many of those who had fought with the IRA for an independent republic found it completely unacceptable. Both Sinn Féin and the IRA split, prompting the Irish Civil War from 1922 to 1923. A timeline of the major actions of the conflict can be found at **https://en.wikipedia.org/wiki/Timeline_of_ the_Irish_Civil_War**. Ultimately, the pro-Treaty side won the war, but it left deep divisions within Irish society for many years to come.

The NAI has been cataloguing Finance Compensation claims under FIN/COMP/2, which deal with claims for any loss of or damage to property as a result of the conflict between July 1921 and March 1923, under the Damage to Property (Compensation) Act of 1923.

Following the Civil War, efforts were made to commemorate the actions of those who had fought for Ireland's freedom. A 1916 medal was created on 24 January 1941 and awarded to those who were recognised

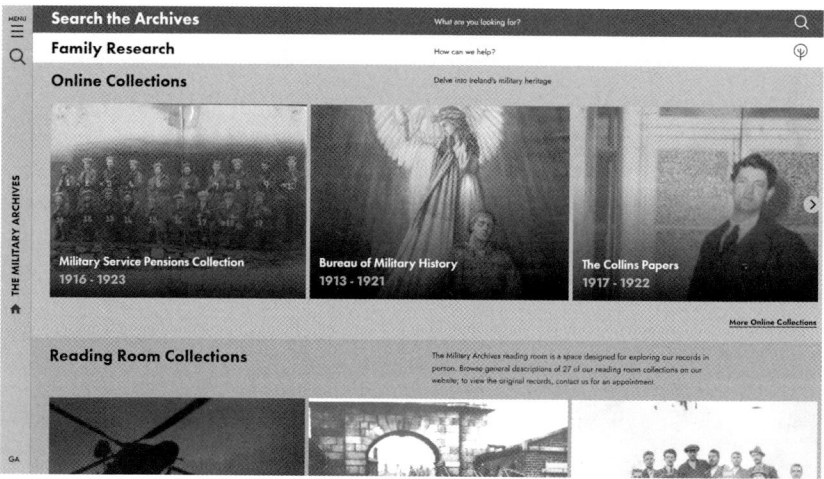

The Military Archives website is invaluable for research into the Easter Rising, the War of Independence, and the Civil War.

as having served during the week commencing 23 April 1916, including awards made posthumously to dependants. Several Army Service Pensions Acts were also passed by the Dáil, dealing with wounded service personnel and deceased participants' dependants.

The names of applicants for medals and pensions for military service between the Easter Rising and September 1924 can be searched through the Military Service Pensions Collection on **MilitaryArchives.ie**. The recipients included members of the Irish Volunteers, the Irish Citizen Army, the IRA, the women's republic organisation Cumann na mBan, Na Fianna Éireann, the Hibernian Army, and the National Army, as well as the Connaught Rangers who mutinied in India in 1920 in protest at the imposition of martial law in Ireland. Additional materials from 1921 to 1923 include nominal roles for the IRA (arranged by division), Cumann na mBan (arranged by county), and Na Fianna Éireann (by county). The same database can be searched at Findmypast.

For those who served in the National Army, a census can be consulted from November 1922. With no census recorded in 1921, a detailed census of serving members of the National Army (*Free State Army*) was carried out on 12/13 November 1922. This was to help the Army Council adequately establish its strength for payment purposes. For each soldier the census records regimental number, rank, corps, surname, forename, age, address, pay book number, the date and place of attestation, marital status, religion, next-of-kin details, and any remarks. As well as being hosted on **MilitaryArchives.ie**, the collection can also be searched through

---

CASE STUDY: A century on from the period of the Easter Rising through to the Civil War, it is possible to reconstruct the activities of many of the republican activists from the many resources that have been opened up to public access as part of the recent Decade of Centenaries commemorations, as the following example will show.

From standard genealogical sources Robert Emmet Kelly was found to have been born in Maginnis Street, Newry, in 1879, to Joseph Kelly and Mary McDonald. Robert became a stonecutter, and later married a Margaret Smyth in Newry in July 1939.

What the civil registration records do not point to is that Robert was heavily involved in the politics of Sinn Féin, and had membership of the IRA, for which he makes frequent appearances in the British Newspaper Archive (p.23), and within the records of the Military Archives. The *Frontier Sentinel* of 13 May 1916, just two weeks after the Easter Rising in Dublin, details how Robert was first arrested at a Sinn Féin meeting in Newry (*Frontier Sentinel* (1916). Arrests in Newry. 13 May. p.5), with the *Irish Times* produced '*Sinn Féin Rebellion Handbook*' (p.144), further noting in its 'Prisoners Deported and Released' section that he was one of 273 prisoners removed from Richmond Barracks on 12 May 1916 and lodged in Wakefield Detention Barracks a day later, with the book confirming his address in Newry and his occupation as a stonecutter.

Less than a year later, on Monday, 17 September 1917, the *Belfast News-Letter* described how Robert had chaired a Sinn Féin meeting in Newry, at which the president of Sinn Féin himself, Arthur Griffiths, made an address (*Belfast News-Letter* (1917). Sinn Fein Meeting at Newry. 17 September. p.3). On 19 August Robert, by now president of Newry Trades Council, was further noted in the *Derry Journal* as having been arrested while attending a Sinn Féin meeting (*Derry Journal* (1918). Another Round Up – Many Arrests Follow on Sinn Fein Meetings. 19 August. p.3), confirmed by Findmypast's 'Easter Rising & Ireland Under Martial Law 1916–1921' collection, which adds that he was then court-martialled in Belfast by the British on 6 September 1918, and was found guilty of offences against the defence of the realm for which he was sentenced to six months' imprisonment with hard labour.

Following his release, Robert stood in the general election in Newry on behalf of Sinn Féin (*Newry Reporter* (1921). Another Round Up – Many Arrests Follow on Sinn Fein Meetings. 19 August. p.3). Following Partition just a few months later, he was then noted to be the president of Sinn Féin's South Down Comhairle Ceanntair ('District Council' in the Irish language) at a meeting in January 1922, at which a motion was discussed to have the Boundary Commission redraw the boundary of Northern Ireland, so that Newry could join the new Irish Free State (*Derry Journal* (1918). S. Down and S. Armagh. 19 August. p.3). The *Belfast News-Letter* of 29 September 1924 describes Robert's further arrest in Newry after the Irish Civil War, during which he had been interned as a member of the anti-Treaty wing of the IRA. The article notes his address at this point as being in County Louth, just over the border from the new state of Northern Ireland (*Belfast News-Letter* (1924). Newry Incident. 29 September. p.8).

A more comprehensive account of Robert's experiences during this period is available from the Military Service Pensions Collection from the Military Archives platform (p.143), which confirms that Robert joined the IRA, and received a pension later in life as an active

> service member of 2 Brigade's 4th Northern Division, 2nd Battalion (Source: File Reference MSP34REF2857).
>
> A summary of his military service is also included on the site, which notes that he had joined the Irish Republican Brotherhood in 1904 and had organised for them in counties Armagh and Down. During the War of Independence, he took part in an arms raid on Ballyedmond Castle in 1919, a raid on the Customs House in Newry in 1920, organised railway workers in Newry to strike and refuse to carry British Army munitions on their trains that same summer, helped to establish the Republican courts in County Down and acted as district justice, and stood as a candidate in the 'Urban Elections' in Newry that year. He narrowly escaped being killed at home by a 'murder gang' in spring 1921.
>
> During the Civil War Robert fought on the anti-Treaty side, and was promoted to Battalion Intelligence Officer of the 2nd Battalion, 2 Brigade IRA, after which he was arrested by National Army forces and interned in Dundalk and Newbridge until 1923. The files include several witness statements backing up his claims.
>
> Also on the Military Archives site, within the Bureau of Military History interviews, are handwritten notes by Robert detailing his involvement, made just prior to his death in 1949.

third party indexes on Ancestry ('Web: Ireland, National Army Census, 1922') and on Findmypast ('Irish Army Census 1922'). The site also holds further collections, such as the 'Civil War Internment Collection' and 'Civil War Operations and Intelligence Reports Collections'.

The Legacy of Conflict

Despite the end of the Civil War, the 'Old IRA', as it is known today, continued to agitate for decades against the Irish Free State – which eventually became recognised internationally as the Republic of Ireland from April 1949 – as well as in Northern Ireland and mainland Britain. It was heavily repressed during the Second World War (known as the 'Emergency' in neutral Ireland at that point), and in the aftermath of its failed 'Border Campaign' of the 1950s, in which it tried to attack the military infrastructure along the border with Northern Ireland, it became a much diminished force.

The civil rights politics of Northern Ireland would later see it largely replaced in the late 1960s by a new 'Provisional IRA', which went on to fight against the Royal Ulster Constabulary, the British Army, Stormont,

Westminster, and Northern Irish based 'loyalist' paramilitaries. This deadly thirty-year conflict, called 'The Troubles', finally came to an end with a ceasefire in 1994. For an overview, Wesley Johnston's pages on The Troubles from 1969 to 1998 at **www.wesleyjohnston.com/users/ireland/past/troubles/index.htm** are a useful resource, while some forty-two editions of the Belfast History Project's publication *The Troubles: A Chronology of the Northern Ireland Conflict* can be freely accessed as downloadable PDF documents from **https://web.archive.org/web/20230201205052/http://www.belfasthistoryproject.com/the-troubles/**.

The Conflict Archive on the Internet (CAIN) is located at **https://cain.ulster.ac.uk/cain**, with various databases and resources, while PRONI has a tie in project at **www.nidirect.gov.uk/articles/proni-records-cain**, which includes a searchable database of records held at the facility. PRONI also offers guidance on how to search court records and inquest records.

For those imprisoned, interned or working in Northern Ireland's prisons in the conflict, the Prisons Memory Archive at **https://prisonsmemoryarchive.com** has a series of a thousand pictures and 175 interviews recorded at Armagh Gaol, the Maze Prison, and Long Kesh Prison, from 2006–7. Initially recorded as the Prisons Audio Visual Archive, the interviewees include staff, probation officers, prisoners, chaplains, teachers and visitors with stories from the Troubles period.

FURTHER READING

BARDON, Jonathan, (1992) *A History of Ulster* Belfast, Blackstaff Press.
BETTINGER, Blaine, (2016) *The Family Tree Guide to DNA Testing and Genetic Genealogy: How to Harness the Power of DNA to Advance Your Family Tree Research* Cincinnati, Family Tree Books.
BLACK, Lynsey, (2024) *Gender and punishment in Ireland: Women, murder and the death penalty, 1922–64* Manchester, Manchester University Press.
CLEARY, Caitriona, (2007) *Social Change and Everyday Life in Ireland 1850–1922* Manchester, Manchester University Press.
COEN, Mark, O'DONNELL, Katherine, et al (2022) *The Dublin Magdalene Laundry: Donnybrook and Church-State Power in Ireland* Bloomsbury Academic.
CONNOLLY, S.J., (2011) *The Oxford Companion to Irish History* Oxford, Oxford University Press.
ESTES, Roberta, (2024) *The Complete Guide to Family Tree DNA: Y-DNA, Mitochondrial, and Autosomal and X-DNA* Baltimore, Genealogical Publishing Company.
FOWLER, Simon, (2017) *Tracing Your Army Ancestors (3rd edition)*. Barnsley, Pen and Sword Books Ltd.
FOY, Michael T. and BARTON, Brian, (2011) *The Easter Rising* History Press.
GRENHAM, John, (2019) *Tracing Your Irish Ancestors (5th edition)* Dublin, Gill Books Ltd.
GURRIN, Brian, (2021) *People, Place and Power: The Grand Jury System in Ireland* Dublin, Trinity College Dublin.
HERBER, Mark, (2005) *Ancestral Trails* Sparkford, Sutton Publishing Ltd.
HOLTON, Graham S., (ed.) (2019) *Tracing Your Ancestors Using DNA: A Guide for Family Historians* Barnsley, Pen and Sword Books Ltd.
HOPKINSON, Michael, (2004) *The Irish War of Independence: The Definitive Account of the Anglo Irish War of 1919–1921* Gill & McMillan.
KELLY, Fergus, (1988) *A Guide to Early Irish Law* Dublin, Dublin Institute for Advanced Studies.
KENNA, G.B., (1997) *Facts and Figures of the Belfast Pogrom 1920–1922* Edinburgh, Luath Press.

LUDDY, Maria, and O'DOWD, Mary, (2020) *Marriage in Ireland 1660–1925* Cambridge, Cambridge University Press.

MAGUIRE, Roderick, (2013) *The People's Courts: Ireland's Dail Courts, 1920–24*, CreateSpace Independent Publishing Platform.

MAUGER, Alice, (2018) *The Cost of Insanity in Nineteenth-Century Ireland: Public Voluntary and Private Asylum Care* London, Palgrave MacMillan.

MITCHELL, Brian, (2002) *A New Genealogical Atlas of Ireland (2nd ed.)* Genealogical Publishing Co., Inc.

PATON, Chris, (2021) *Sharing Your Family History Online: A Guide for Family Historians* Barnsley, Pen and Sword Family History.

PATON, Chris, (2019) *Tracing Your Scottish Ancestry Through Church and State Records*, Pen and Sword Family History.

REDMOND, Paul Jude, (2018) *The Adoption Machine: The Dark History of Ireland's Mother & Baby Homes and the Inside Story of How 'Tuam 800' Became a Global Scandal* Dublin, Merrion Press.

ROE, Mark B., (2022) *The Least of These: The Tragic Story of Dublin's Foundling Hospital* Dublin, The History Press Ireland.

ROULSTON, William J., (2020) *Researching Presbyterian Ancestors in Ireland* Belfast, Ulster Historical Foundation.

ROULSTON, William J., (2018) *Researching Ulster Ancestors: The Essential Genealogical Guide to Early Modern Ulster, 1600–1800* Belfast, Ulster Historical Foundation.

RYAN, James G., (ed.) (2001) *Irish Church Records* Dublin, Flyleaf Press.

SCOTT, Brendan, and DOOHER, John, (ed.) (2013) *Plantation: Aspects of Seventeenth Century Ulster Society* Belfast, Ulster Historical Foundation & Ulster Local History Trust.

SMITH, James M., (2022) *Ireland's Magdalen Laundries and the Nation's Architecture of Containment*, University of Notre Dame Press.

URQUHART, Diane, (2020) *Irish Divorce: A History* Cambridge, Cambridge University Press.

YOUNG, Robert M., (2008) *Town Book of the Corporation of Belfast* Belfast, Colourpoint Books.

INDEX

10th and 16th (Irish) Divisions, 140
1641 Depositions, 126–9
36th (Ulster) Division, 140

a mensa et thoro, 57, 59–61
abortion, xvii, 31, 56
Act for the Registration of Births and Deaths, 1863, 32
Act of Settlement, 1652, 130
Act of Supremacy, 1558, 124
Act of Union, 1800, 78, 131
Adopted Children Register (ROI), 50
adoption, ix, xvi, xvii, 25, 31, 41–2, 49–50, 63, 78
Adoption Act (ROI), 1952, xvii, 50–1
Adoption of Children Act (NI), 1929, xvi, 49
Adoption (Northern Ireland) Order, 1987, 49
Adoption Contact Register (NI), 49
Adoption Search Reunion, 49
Adoption Rights Now, 41
adultery, 54, 56–60
Adventurers, 130
An tÓglach, 145
Ancestry, 5, 8–11, 19–20, 91, 94–6, 118, 133, 135, 144, 147
Anglican Record Project, 7
Anglo-Irish Treaty, 1921, xvi, 99, 146, 148–9
Antrim, viii, xiv, 65, 68–9, 74, 83–4, 87–8, 106, 118, 125–7

Áras an Uachtaráin, 38
arbitration, 76, 82, 134
archives, xi, xii, xvii, 1, 7–9, 11–15, 25, 47–8, 51–2, 54, 61, 67–8, 78, 80–1, 84, 89–90, 93, 95, 100, 109–10, 117, 123, 126, 131, 133, 136–7, 140, 143–50
Armagh, 9, 25, 60, 68, 74, 83, 85–7, 118, 125, 136, 148–50
Armagh Gaol, 150
Army Service Pensions Acts, 146
Ascendancy, Protestant, 130
Ask About Ireland, 16
assizes, 55, 61–2, 69, 78–9, 83–4, 131
asylums, xiv, 34–7, 40, 47, 93, 118–23
Australia, 34, 45, 51–2, 93–6, 108, 132

Ballinasloe, 118
Ballycastle, 84
Ballyedmond Castle, 149
Bank of Ireland, 38
bankruptcy, 79, 133, 139
banns, 52–3
Baptist Church, 5, 62
bastards, xiv, 29–30, 33, 105–106, 108
Belfast, viii, xvii, 2, 4, 7, 9, 13, 17–20, 23–5, 27, 33, 34, 38, 49, 56, 58, 60, 68–74, 81, 85, 88–9, 91, 103, 106–15, 117–18, 137–8, 145, 148, 150
Belfast, Town Book of the Corporation of, 112
Belfast Central Library, 17, 23

Belfast Charitable Society, 103, 113
Belfast Corporation, 112, 117
Belfast Newsletter, 19, 58, 70, 148
Bermuda, 48
Betham, Sir William, 9
Bettinger, Blaine, 11, 151
bigamy, 57, 61–3
Bill, William, 69–70
Birth Information and Tracing Act (ROI), 2022, xvii, 42
births, x, xv, xvii, 1–2, 4, 17–19, 22, 29–33, 40, 42, 48–50, 92, 106
bishops, 52, 64, 126
Black and Tans, 145
Black Diaries, 65
Board of Commissioners in Lunacy, 118
boards of guardians, 19, 31, 47, 104–105, 107, 109, 133
body fine, 76
Books of Survey and Distribution, 130
Bon Secours Mother and Baby Home, 42
Bord Uchtála, An, 49
Boston, 132
Bray, 62, 93
breach of promise, 55
Brehon law, 56, 75–7, 96
bridewells, 92
Britainxv, 7, 8, 30–1, 34, 38, 43, 50–1, 60, 64, 77–8, 93, 96, 101, 104, 110–11, 113, 118, 125–6, 131–3, 138, 144–5, 149
British Army, 103, 116, 136, 140–2, 144–5, 149
British Expeditionary Force, 141
British Library, 17, 22–3, 54
British Newspaper Archive, 23, 94, 138, 147
Brown, Robert, 127–9
Burke, Sir John Bernard, 9
buckle the beggars, 53
Bureau of Military History, 143, 149
burial, 5, 6, 19–20, 36, 41–2, 69

calendars, probate, 9, 19–20
Canada, 34, 47, 51–2, 132

canon law, 56
capital offences, 62, 96–101
Carlow, 6, 7, 22, 62, 78, 118, 120–1
Carrick-on-Suir, 33, 94, 109, 116, 134, 141
Carrickfergus, viii, 125, 128–9
Carrigan, Rev. William, 9
Carson, Edward, 136
Casement, Sir Roger, 65
Castlebar, 118
Castlepollard, 41
Catholic Parish Registers at the NLI, 5
Catholic Qualification Rolls, 131
Catholic Relief Act, 1793, xiv–xv, 131
Catholic Rotunda Girl's Aid Society, 34
Cavan, 37, 109, 125
censuses, xv–xvi, 1, 7–8, 18, 20–1, 30–1, 133, 147
Central Mental Hospital, 123
Chancery, 79–80
Chapelizod, 47
Chicago, 132
child migrants, 51–2
Children's Homes, 38, 43, 47
cholera, Asiatic, 113–15
Church of Ireland, xvi, 5, 7, 34, 46–8, 52–4, 57–8, 62, 87, 89, 106–107, 124, 131, 133
Church of Jesus Christ of Latter-day Saints, 54
church courts, 56, 87–9
church records, 1, 4–7, 14, 33, 89
civil partnerships, 63
civil registration, xv, 1–2, 4, 17, 19, 22, 32, 106–107, 117, 147
civil rights, 149
Civil War, xi, xvi, 1, 25, 68, 82, 109, 136, 146–9
Clare, 19, 62, 87, 109
Clare, Wallace, 9
Cleary, John, 11
Clifton House, 103
Cloncurry, Baron and Baroness, 58–9
Clonmel, 94–5, 118, 142
Colleton, Martin, 141

Colleton, Mary Ann and Margaret, 116
commercial researchers, 26–7
Commission of Investigation into Mother and Baby Homes and Certain Related Matters, xvii, 42
Conflict Archive on the Internet (CAIN), 150
Connolly, James, 90, 138–9
Connolly, Dr. Philomena, 80
consanguinity, 56
conscription crisis, 144
consistorial courts, 88
Contact Preference Register, 42
convicts (transported), 61, 94–6
Cornwall, Gustavus, 66
Cork, 6, 34, 38, 45, 55, 61, 87, 104, 111, 114, 119, 122, 133, 137
coroners, ix, 68, 71
Council of Irish Genealogical Organisations, 25
couple beggars, 53–4, 61
Courtney, Robert, 72–4
Court of Exchequer, 80
Court of King's Bench, 79
court baron, 85–6
court leet, 84–5
courts, 78–89
courts martial, 97, 99, 144
Cousins, Margaret, 137
Craig, James, 136
crime, x, xi, 34, 61–2, 64, 66, 70–1, 75, 81, 90–8, 101, 123, 140, 143
criminal conversation, xvii, 56, 58, 60
Criminal Justice Act (Northern Ireland), 1966, 71
Criminal Law Amendment Act, 1885, 65
Criminal Law (Ireland) Act, 1828, 96
Criminal Law (Sexual Offences), 1993, 67
Criminal Law (Suicide) Act, 1993, 71
Criminal Lunatics (Ireland), 1838, 123
Cromwell, Oliver, xiv, 124, 130
Crosslé, Philip, 9
Crumlin Road Gaol, 91, 101

Cumann na mBan, 26, 67, 147
Currie, Jean, viii

D'Arcy, Henry, 107
Dáil courts, 82, 97
Dáil Éireann, xvi, 16, 82, 97, 144–6
Damage to Property (Compensation) Act, 1923, 146
death penalty, x, 64, 71, 96–7, 99
deaths, 1–2, 4, 17, 22, 30, 32, 45, 68, 107, 113–14, 116–17, 122
Declaration of Loyalty, 135
denization, 125–6
Denny House, 40
deportation (from Britain), 110–12
deserted children, 37, 48, 108
dioceses, 54, 88–9
Discovery (catalogue), 15, 143
Disenfranchising Act, 1727, 131
dispensaries, 113, 115
divorces, xiv, xvi–xvii, 56–62, 76
DNA, x–xi, 2, 9–11, 20, 22, 31
domestic service, 29
Donegal, 19, 82, 84, 114, 125
Donnelly, Brian, 68, 117
Donovan, Johanna, 33, 109
Down, xiv, 9, 68, 74, 83, 88, 95, 112, 114, 125, 136, 148–9
Down County Museum, 95–6
Down Survey, 130
Downpatrick, 95, 118, 125
Drogheda, 37, 130
Drumcondra, 36
Drummond School, 47
Dublin, xiv, xvii, 1–2, 4, 6–7, 9, 11–16, 18–19, 22, 24–6, 33, 36–40, 43, 44–8, 51–2, 54, 58, 60–1, 63, 66–8, 75, 77–80, 82, 84, 87, 89–90, 92–4, 97–9, 103, 109, 113–15, 118–19, 125–9, 132, 136–40, 142–6
Dublin Castle, 15, 66, 90, 119, 136, 142–3
Dublin Commission Court, 79, 97
Dublin Corporation, 114
Dublin District Coroner's Court, 68
Dublin Foundling Hospital, xiv, 43–5

Dublin Hospital Girls Aid Association, 34
Dublin Lockout, 48, 90, 138–40
Dublin Magdalene Asylum, xiv, 34
Dublin Metropolitan Police, 48, 89–90, 139–40, 143–5
Dublin United Tramway Company, 138
Dublin Women's Suffrage Society, 137
Dúchas Project, The, 14
Duke of York's Royal Military School, 47
Dundalk, 149
Dunluce, 84

Earl Grey Pauper Immigration Scheme, 51, 108
Easter Rising, xvi, 15, 65, 67, 97, 108, 140, 142–4, 147–8
emancipation, Catholic, xv, 5, 35, 131
Encumbered Estates Acts, xv, 79, 133
English law, 75, 77–9, 96, 124
Ennis, 118
Enniscorthy, 118
Enniskeen, 37
epidemics, 102, 113, 115, 117
European Court of Human Rights, 67
eyres, 79
executions, 96–101, 143–4

fallen women, 34–9
families, ix, xi, 2, 7–8, 28, 30–1, 34, 63, 67, 71, 75–8, 90–1, 106, 109, 118, 128, 133
Family Law Act, 1981, xvii, 60
FamilySearch, 8–9, 13, 54, 81, 92, 134
FamilyTreeDNA, 10
Famine, Great, xv, 2, 35, 42, 47, 51, 79, 105, 115, 131–4
Famine Relief Commission, 133
fathers, 4, 29, 47
Federation for Ulster Local Studies Limited, 25
Federation of Local History Societies, 26

fee farm, 125
fee simple, 125
felo de se (suicide), 71, 74
Fermanagh, 31, 68, 83, 125, 136
Fianna Éireann, Na, 141, 147
Findmypast, 6, 8–9, 13, 17–20, 23–4, 27, 47–8, 51, 82, 84, 89–90, 92–3, 96, 109–10, 126, 134–5, 137, 140, 144–5, 147–8
First World War, xvi, 8, 103, 116, 137, 140–1
Flight of the Earls, xiv, 79, 125
forfeiture of land, 76, 130
foundlings, ix, 43–5, 103
Four Courts, xvi, 1, 8–9, 13, 22, 59, 75, 78–81, 93
Fowler, Simon, 141
France, 61, 141
Free State of Ireland (Saorstát Éireann), xiv, xvi–xvii, 8, 33, 49, 52, 60, 80–2, 84, 89, 97, 99–100, 109, 117, 143, 146–9

Galway, 19, 35–6, 38, 42, 136, 137
Garda Síochána, An, 71, 89–90, 100
gateway sites, 11–12
Genealogical Society of Ireland, 25
General Post Office, 66, 142
General Register Office (GRO), 2, 4, 22, 50, 54
General Register Office for Northern Ireland, 3–4, 49
Germany, 61, 136
Gibson, Mary Jane, 108
Giles, Henry, 33
Gillespie, Margaret, 111
Gillespie, Raymond, 87
Glasgow, 31, 114
Glasnevin Cemetery, 11, 36, 67, 142
Glenarm, 84
Glorious Revolution, 130
Good Shepherd Sisters, 35
Gordon, Margaret, 106
Gordon, Mary, 105–106
Gorta Mór, An, xv, 131
Government of Ireland Act, 1920, xvi, 80, 145
Graham, Ernest, viii–ix, xiii

grand juries, 79, 81, 83–4, 115, 118
Greene, Michael and John, 94–5
Greenwich Union, 111
Grenan, Julie, 67
Grenham, John, 12, 89
Grosse Île Quarantine Station, 47
Guinness, 38
Gurrin, Brian, 84

Haan, J., 61
Haigh, Roland, 62
Halliday, Alexander William, 48, 139
Hamilton, James, xiv, 125
Hampstead House, 119
Hansard, 81
Haslam, Anna, 137
health, 30, 34, 41–2, 55, 72, 102–103, 106–107, 112–18, 121
Hibernian Army, 147
Higginbotham, Peter, 32, 38, 40, 43, 47, 104
High Court, Northern Ireland, 60, 80
Highfield House, 119
Holywell, 118
home children, xvi, 45, 51–2
home rule, 116, 135–7, 140
Homosexual Offences (Northern Ireland) Order, 1982, 67
homosexuality, 56, 63–7
Honourable The Irish Society, The, 125
honour price, 76
Horrigan, Mary, 111
hospitals, 112–18
Huntingdon Library, 80

illegitimacy, ix, xvii, 29–43, 49–50, 104–105
illness, 55, 67, 102, 116, 118–19
industrial schools, 38, 47
infanticide, 30
infertility, 56
influenza, 102, 116
Interments (felo de se) Act, 1882, 74
Internet Archive, xii, 11, 123, 140, 145
Irish Archives Resource, 14

Irish Army, 38, 147
Irish Citizen Army, 139–40, 142–3, 145, 147
Irish Family History Centre, 26–7
Irish Family History Foundation, 20, 25–6
Irish Genealogical Research Society, 25
Irish Labour Party, 138
Irish Manuscripts Commission, 9, 130
Irish Newspaper Archives, 23
Irish Parliamentary Party, 35, 136
Irish Queer Archive, 67
Irish Reproductive Loan Fund, 110
Irish Republican Army (IRA), xvii, 97, 99–100, 141, 145–9
Irish Republican Brotherhood, 136, 149
Irish Republican Police, 82
Irish Transport and General Workers Union (ITGWU), 138
Irish Volunteers, 136, 140, 142–3, 145, 147
Irish Women's Franchise League, 137
Irish Women's Suffrage and Local Government Association, 137
Irish Women's Suffrage Foundation, 137
Irish Women's Suffrage Society, 137
Irish Women's Workers' Union, 138
IrishGenealogy.ie, 3–4, 6–7, 21
Irvinestown, 107
Islandmagee, 106–107, 126–7
Isle of Man, 59

James I, 77, 125
Johnston, Wesley, 133, 149
Judgment of Death Act, 1823, 96
Justice for Magdalenes, 38
justices of the peace, 31, 79, 81–2, 105

Keefe, Mary, 120
Kelly, Fergus, 77
Kelly, Joseph, 98–9, 147
Kelly, Robert Emmet, 147

Kerry, 6–7
Kildare, 22, 29, 58, 77
Kilkenny, 46, 77, 87, 114, 116, 118
Killaloe, 54, 62
Killarney, 118
Killonerry, 134
Kilmainham, 92–3, 100, 119, 143–4
King's Court, 78
kirk sessions, 33, 56–7, 88–9
Kirwan House, 46
Knockbracken Mental Health Services, 118

Lancashire Record Office, 110
Land Commission Advances, 135
Land Judges Court, 133
Land Law (Ireland) Act, 1881, 134
Land War, xvi, 134–5
Landed Estates Court Rentals, 134
Langtry, Margaret, 69–70
Laois, xiv, 22, 78, 124
Larkin, Jim, 90, 138–9
Larne, 25, 72–3, 83, 106–107, 136
Last Chance to Read, 91
Lawless, Lord Valentine Brown, 58–9
Legitimacy Act, 1931, xvi, 28
Legitimacy Act (Northern Ireland), 1928, xvi, 28
lesbianism, 67
Letterkenny, 118
Levin, John, 81
Library and Archives Canada, 51–2
Limerick, 36, 38, 87, 99, 104, 118, 123, 137
Linen Hall Library, 17
Liverpool, 110, 115, 138
Lloyd, Constance, 63
Local Government (Ireland) Act, 1898, 68
local government boards, 116
Loftus, Daniel, 42–3
Londonderry, 9, 19, 51, 68, 83, 118, 125, 138
Long Kesh Prison, 150
lordship of Ireland, 77–8, 84
Louth, 77, 84, 114, 148
Lowtherstown, 107

Luddy, Maria, 56, 63
Lunacy (Ireland) Act, 1821, 118
Lunacy Act, 1845, 119
Lutheran church, 54

Macbeth, Madam, 61
MacDonnell, Randal, Earl of Ulster, 84
McGladdery, Robert, 101
MacPherson, Annie, 51
Magdalene laundries/asylums, xvii, 34–9
Magdalene Names Project, 38
Magdalene Oral History Project, 38
Magee, Bryan, 127–8
Manning, Michael, 99
manor records, 84–7
Marriage (Ireland) Act, 1844, 53–4
Marriage Act, 2015, 63
marriages, xv, xvii, 1–2, 4–6, 11, 17–19, 22, 33, 52–7, 59–63, 76, 78, 87, 104, 131, 133
marriages, annulment, 56–7
marriages, irregular, 53–4
marriages, mixed, 52–3
marriages, same sex, xvii, 63
martial law, 144, 147–8
Maryborough, 118
Matrimonial Causes Act (Northern Ireland) 1939, xvii, 60
Maze Prison, 150
Maudesly, John Cavendish, 61
Mayo, 113
Medical Charities Act, 1851, 115
mental illness, 118–23
Methodist Church, 5
Military Archives (website), 143, 145–9
Military Service Pensions Collection, 143, 147–8
Monaghan, 37, 118
Mooney, Teresa, 11, 48
Montgomery, Hugh, 125–6
Montgomery, Ian, 87
Moravian Church, 5
Morgan, Eliza Georgiana, 58
Morrow, Frances, 31

mother and baby homes, xvii, 30, 38, 40–3, 49
mothers, viii, ix, x, xvii, 4, 10–11, 29–44, 48–50, 59, 70, 94, 98, 105–106, 127
Movement of Extremists reports, 143
Moving Here (website), 110
Mullingar, 117–18, 141
Munster Women's Franchise League, 137
murder, xiv, 30, 43, 69–71, 76, 96–101, 126–9, 149
Murphy, William Martin, 138
MyHeritage, 8, 10, 22, 92

National Archive of Ireland (NAI), 8, 12–13, 15, 18, 54, 68, 74, 82, 89, 92–3, 95, 109, 123, 131, 133, 137, 143, 146
National Archives (UK), 15, 48, 78, 80, 89–90, 95, 110, 126, 140, 143
National Army, 99, 147, 149
National Centre for Research and Remembrance, 38–9
National Folklore Collection, 14
National Library of Ireland (NLI), xvi, 5–6, 16, 22, 67, 80, 140, 144
National Library of Wales, 15, 17
National Records of Scotland, 15
naturalisation, 125–6
Ne Temere, 53
New Ross, 38, 98
New South Wales, xv, 94–6
New Zealand, 51
Newbridge, 149
Newry, 54, 101, 120, 147–9
newspapers, x, 14, 18–19, 22–4, 56, 68, 70, 72–3, 75, 93–4, 138, 145, 147
Newsplan, 22
Nine Years' War, 124
North of Ireland Family History Society, 10–11, 25
North of Ireland Women's Suffrage Society, 137
Northern Ireland, xiv, xvi, 3–4, 7–8, 13–14, 17, 19–20, 23–6, 31, 33, 38, 42, 47, 49, 52, 60, 63, 67–8, 71, 80, 83–4, 89, 91–2, 96, 101, 109, 117, 123, 145, 148–50
Northern Ireland Historical Institutional Abuse Inquiry, 52

O'Brien, William, 66, 140
O'Donnell, Red Hugh, 124
O'Dowd, Mary, 56, 63
O'Farrell, Elizabeth, 67
O'Kenny, Enda, 34
O'Mahony, S.C., 87
O'Neill, Hugh, 124–5
Offaly, xiv, 78, 124
Offences Against the Person Act, 1829, 64
Offences Against the Person Act, 1861, 64, 96
Old Bailey, 93
Old English, 77–8
Oldstone, 84
Oireachtas Library, 16, 24, 81, 91
Omagh, 118
oral history, ix, 2, 38
Orange Order, 135
orphans, 46–50, 51
oyer and terminer, 79

parish, xv, 2, 5–7, 12, 18–21, 29, 31, 37, 41, 46, 53, 62, 82, 89, 104, 106, 110–12, 126–7
Park House, 46
Parliament, Irish, xv, 24, 30, 60, 63, 77, 78, 81, 113, 118, 125
Parliament, UK, 7–8, 29, 59–61, 81, 84, 96, 110–11, 123, 135–6
Partition (of Ireland), xvi, 3–4, 8, 24, 28, 36, 38, 40, 48, 51–2, 60–1, 67–8, 84, 89, 99, 101, 109, 117, 144–6, 148
Paton, Charles, viii
Peace Preservation Force, 89
Pearse, Patrick, 67, 142–3
Pelletstown, 40
Penal Laws, 5, 96, 130–1
penance, 35–6
pensioners, 72, 105
petty sessions, 18, 31, 79, 81–3
Pierrepoint, Thomas, 99
Piers, Sir John, 59

Plantations of Ulster, xiv, 78, 84, 124–6
police, ix, 36–7, 45, 48, 70, 82, 89–92, 94, 99, 138–45
Police Service of Northern Ireland, 89, 91
Poor Law, ix, xv, 19, 31, 44, 52, 103–12, 115–16, 119, 133
Poor Law (Amendment) Act, 1834 (England/Wales), 104, 110
Poor Law (Amendment) Act, 1862, 115
Poor Relief (Ireland) Act, 1838, xv, 102, 104
poor removals, 110–12
Portadown, 60, 126
Portlaoise Prison, 100
Portrane, 118, 123
Post Office, 66, 142
poverty, x, 102–12, 138
pregnancy, 30–1, 33, 40–1, 106, 120
Prerogative Court, 9, 89
Presbyterian Historical Society of Ireland, 7, 56, 89
Presbyterians, 5, 7, 33–4, 52–3, 56–7, 88–9, 130–1
prisoners, 22, 70, 74, 79, 90, 92, 95–6, 129, 137, 139–40, 143, 148, 150
prisons, 18, 22, 37, 53, 62–5, 70–1, 74, 89, 92–3
Prisons Audio Visual Archive, 150
Prisons Memory Archive, 150
privacy, xi, 8, 14
Private Asylums (Ireland) Act, 1842, 119
Project Infant, 42–3
Property Losses (Ireland) Committee, 143
prostitution, 30, 34, 65
Protestants, 2, 5, 7, 20, 33–4, 43–6, 52–3, 56–7, 65, 67, 87, 126, 130–1, 135, 140
Provisional IRA, 149
Public Health Act, 1878, 115
Public Record Office (PRO), xi, xvi, xvii, 1, 13, 15, 25, 54, 59, 78, 87
Public Record Office of Northern Ireland (PRONI), xvi, xvii, 7, 9, 12, 13–15, 20, 33, 38, 47, 56, 61, 68, 71–4, 83, 85, 87–9, 93, 101, 106, 107–109, 117, 123, 135–6, 138, 150
Purdysburn Villa Colony, 118

quarter sessions, 74, 79, 81–3, 110
Quebec, 47, 51
Queen's University, 42, 81

Raphoe, 82, 89
Raymond's County Down (website), 112
rebellions, xiv, xv, 124, 126–31, 142–4, 148
Redmond, John, 136
reformatories, 38, 40, 47
referendums, 60, 63
Registry of Deeds, xiv, 9
Representative Church Body Library, 33, 89
Republic of Ireland, xiv, xvii, 4, 12, 31, 82, 117, 149
Roche, Eliza, 55
Roman Catholics, xiv, xv, 2, 5–7, 12, 19–21, 33–4, 35–6, 43–7, 52–3, 57, 60, 67, 84, 93, 95, 124, 126–7, 130–1, 145
RootsIreland, 7, 20–1, 25–6
Roulston, William J., 5, 12, 84
Royal Belfast Maternity Hospital, 118
Royal Hibernian Military School, 47–8
Royal Irish Constabulary (RIC), 15, 19, 89–90, 144–5
Royal Ulster Constabulary (RUC), 89, 91, 149
Royal Victoria Hospital, 117–18
Ryan, James G., 5

St. Patrick's Guild, 40
St. Patrick's Hospital for Imbeciles, 119
Salvation Army, 43
sanatoriums, 92
Santry, Claire, 12
Saunders's News-Letter, 61, 97
Schools Collection, The, 14

Schulze, Johann George Frederick, 54
Scotland, viii, 8, 15, 17, 19, 31–2, 50, 66, 111–14, 125–6, 133
ScotlandsPeople, 8
Seanad Éireann, 16
Senchus Már, 75
seneschal, 87
separation, viii, ix, 54, 56–62, 87
servitors, 125
Sheehy-Skeffington, Hannah, 137–8
Silver War Badge, 140
Sinn Féin, 144–8
Sinn Féin courts, 82
Sinn Féin Rebellion Handbook, 144, 148
Sisters of Charity, 35
Sisters of Mercy, 45
Sisters of Our Lady of Charity of Refuge, 35–6, 39
Skibbereen, 111
Sligo, 60, 109, 115, 118
Smyth, Martha, viii
societies, 2, 7, 10, 17, 19, 22, 25–6, 34, 47, 50, 56, 68, 89, 103, 113, 125–6, 137
Somme Hospital, 117
South Africa, 51, 72
South Dublin Poorhouse, 45
Southern Ireland, xvi, 80, 145–6
Southern Reporter and Cork Commerical Courier, 55
Spanish Flu, 103, 116–17
State Library of Victoria, 52
Status of Children Act (ROI), 1987, xvii, 33
Statute Law Revision Act (ROI), 1983, 78
Statutes of Kilkenny, 77
Statutes Project blog, 81
Stormont, 42, 52, 81, 145, 149
Strain, Robert, 82
Suffrage Map, PRONI, 138
suffragettes, 137–8
suicide, 71–4
Supreme Court of Judicature Act (Ireland) Act of 1877, 80
Swift, Jonathan, 119

syncope, 102
tack 'ems, 53
Tametsi, 53
Templepatrick, 69–70, 88
TheGenealogist (website), 8, 21–2, 96
Tipperary, 11, 22, 33, 87, 94, 109, 116, 134, 142
Toronto, 51, 132
townland, 2, 4, 82, 104, 106, 108, 131
Towns Improvement Act, 1854, 115
transportation, xvi, 53, 61–2, 75, 93–6
Treason Act 1939, 99
Trinity College Dublin, 84, 126–9
Troubles, The, xvii, 68, 71, 75, 117, 149–50
Tuam, 42, 54
tuberculosis, 102, 115, 117
Tusla (Child and Family Agency), 50
typhus, 113, 115
Tyrconnell, 124–5
Tyrone, 25, 68, 83, 85, 124–5

Ulster, xiv, xvi, 7, 12, 18, 20, 25, 27, 34, 42, 78, 84, 87, 92, 124, 124–6, 130, 135–6, 140, 144
Ulster Covenant, xvi, 14, 20, 135
Ulster Historical Foundation, 5, 12, 27, 87, 126
Ulster Unionist Council, 135–6
Ulster University, 42
Ulster Volunteer Force (UVF), 116, 136, 140
UK Parliamentary Papers (ProQuest), 61, 81, 84, 110–12
undertakers, 125–6
Unionists, 135, 136, 144–5
United States (USA), 2, 11, 31, 34, 49, 80
University College Cork, 133

vesting orders, 135
vestries, 89
Virtual Records Treasury of Ireland, 13
vital records, vii, 22

Walker, Mary, 62
War of Independence, xvi, 8, 82, 97, 109, 144–6, 149
Wars of the Three Kingdoms, 124, 130
Waterford, 38, 77, 109, 118, 137
Wellcome Library, 114–15, 117
West Clare, 87
West Sussex Record Office, 87
Westmeath, 58, 117
Westminster Confession of Faith, 57
Wexford, 22, 98
Wicklow, 46, 62
Wilde, Oscar, 63

wills and testaments, 8–9, 14, 19–20, 133
witches, x
Wodsworth, William Dudley, 43–4
Wood, Joseph, 54
women, 10, 30–1, 34–43, 56, 62, 67, 76, 103, 121, 135–8
workhouses, 19, 25, 31–2, 34, 36, 38, 40, 42–4, 47, 51, 67, 73, 102,–109, 115, 117–19, 131, 133, 142
Workhouses (website), 32, 104
Wright, John and Isabella, 60

zymotic diseases, 113–14

Dear Reader,

We hope you have enjoyed this book, but why not share your views on social media? You can also follow our pages to see more about our other products: facebook.com/penandswordbooks or follow us on X @penswordbooks

You can also view our products at www.pen-and-sword.co.uk (UK and ROW) or www.penandswordbooks.com (North America).

To keep up to date with our latest releases and online catalogues, please sign up to our newsletter at: www.pen-and-sword.co.uk/newsletter

If you would like a printed catalogue with our latest books, then please email: enquiries@pen-and-sword.co.uk or telephone: 01226 734555 (UK and ROW) or email: uspen-and-sword@casematepublishers.com or telephone: (610) 853-9131 (North America).

We respect your privacy and we will only use personal information to send you information about our products.

Thank you!